CRAWLING ON THE HIGHWAY

Amira Choukair Tame

First paperback printing June 2020

Printed in the U.S.A

Dedication

I dedicate this book to anyone traveling the road to their unknown future. With an uncertain destination and a dream to succeed, you must keep crawling. If you have a vision of achieving greatness, moving forward is your only option.

I also dedicate "Crawling on the Highway" to all of the students and staff at Wayne County Community College in Detroit, Michigan, who helped me traverse the rocky road ahead of me. They helped make my dream a reality. My African-American friends treated me like family. I truly appreciate all the help they provided as I struggled to the finish line.

Hopefully, after reading this book, you will be inspired to never give up, even in the face of near-death. I hope it gives you strength in the face of adversity. Maybe, someday, you will be an inspiration to others struggling on their life's highway. If I can make it, you can too. Never, never, never give up!

I will donate $1.00 to the WCCC scholarship fund for every book sold to help as they pave the way to their own destinies.

- Amira Choukair Tame

Prologue

When we are born, one of the first things we learn to do is crawl. It is our only method of movement. Soon, we gain the ability to walk. Walking allows us to reach places we want to go much faster than crawling. But what if you were never encouraged to walk? Imagine being stuck in a permanent state of crawling and not allowed to walk. You would never learn to run.

My story starts in a small mountain village in Souane, Lebanon, and ends in a south Florida suburb. The in-betweens are what molded me into the woman I am today. Through the endurance of a strict, often abusive father, a delicate, loving mother, and five siblings with five distinct  personalities, I never complained. I never stopped moving. With my hands and feet planted firmly on the ground, I applied the only motion that has ever felt comfortable to me. I crawled forward as hard as I could. I knew I would be free to fly to higher places someday.

At times, my goals seemed more like nightmares, filled with unforeseen obstacles and speed bumps as large as mountains in the road. Below my feet it felt like a treacherous swamp, with hungry alligators and venomous snakes waiting to lap me up. I thought that if my health held up, I would have the strength to continue. Unfortunately, it didn't hold up. Working three jobs to support myself, going to school full-time, eating poorly, and not getting enough sleep finally took its toll on my body. I couldn't take time off to attend to the pains in my stomach until admitted to the ER on a gurney. I was in and out of emergency rooms many times. Eventually, I developed Crohn's disease, and it was ravaging my insides. I hid the constant, stabbing pains so I wouldn't lose my jobs. How was I going to make it? "Please don't let me die," I begged the ER doctors.

They assured me they wouldn't let me die. I had come too far on my highway to die now.

I have carried with me the baggage of fear, anger, and lack of confidence from my younger years throughout my adult life. It felt like a ball and chain were holding me back. I was a prisoner of my inner self. Fear is something that will always be with me. Fear of not understanding something, fear of being wrong about something, and fear of going the wrong way consumed my every thought. Anxiety and fear rippled throughout my veins continually. If fear of my abusive Dad or abusive teachers wasn't enough, there is more.

When I immigrated to America in 1981, I believed I left my reasons to be afraid back in Lebanon. There was no one to threaten me with punishment if I didn't follow orders to the tee. There was no one to pick me up by my hair and throw me to the floor if I didn't understand something right away. No one to call me dummy...that I didn't deserve to eat...that it was better to give my food to the animals.

Omar, my husband, is an angel and is always there for me. Even after I pledged not to write any more books, he did not let my dream to write a book about my life story die. "Let me get it out of my system. God, don't let me die before I tell my stories," I begged. "Amira! You will tell your stories someday," he assured me.

One day, Omar bought a book for me at an estate sale. The book was authored by Ken Brown. I enjoyed reading about his struggle to achieve success in life. I liked that he was a very religious man. I asked Omar if he could get the author's phone number. I hoped he would be willing to give me advice about writing my book. Omar went back to the estate sale and got Ken's cell phone number. I was so excited, I called him right away. I asked if we could meet to discuss business. Surprisingly, he agreed. I felt he was the right person to help me with my writing. I believe God sent me an angel through Ken Brown. I could see he had a profoundly spiritual heart and a caring soul. This book would not have been possible without my collaboration with Ken Brown and his team, and I sincerely thank him for that.

Chapter 1
My Parents

Mom

My Mom was an amazing lady. She looked like an angel, with long, flowing, black hair and olive-colored skin. The glow in her instantly brightened any room. She was a petite woman, at 5' 2" and less than 110 pounds. Mom had beautiful eyes and a friendly smile. Even when she had the worst day of her life, she still smiled. Because she always smiled, I think it gave the impression that she was a happy woman. But it was not a true impression and didn't reflect her underlying feelings.

Mom's kindness and spirit resonated with everyone she crossed paths with. Her friends and neighbors, even animals, adored her. Mom was born into a very wealthy family in Lebanon. They had money, prestige, and political influence. Because she was the only girl in her family, they treated her well. Her father was a kind and gentle person who treated others with respect and kindness, and her Mom was quiet and didn't show much emotion.

When Mom was 22 years old, a handsome man from a middle class family asked her father if he could marry her. Her father liked the man, so he agreed, even though the suitor could not offer any wealth or status to the family. That man was my Dad.

Mom was already in love with a nice, good-looking man who lived nearby. They didn't date. Dating before marriage was forbidden in our culture. Instead, Mom and the young man would see each other at the store randomly, and they would talk there. Sadly, he got cancer at a young age and died suddenly. My mother's first love was gone. Even though my Mom wasn't interested in marrying anyone else, she agreed to my father's proposal because she didn't care anymore. Internally, she continued to grieve for the one she truly loved. After they were married, Mom was anything but happy because my Dad did not treat her with respect. He believed he was the boss, and she had to obey his every command.

Years later, my Mom had a dream about her first love. He came to her while she was in a deep slumber. "There is an owl," he whispered in her ear, "If you had burned an owl and put the owl's feather on my wound, it would have healed my cancer."

"I wanted you to know," he continued, "if ever someone has cancer, they can get healed. I wish they healed me that way." Had he given my mother a cure for cancer? That was the only time she dreamed of him.

I learned about my Mom's connection with animals at an early age. We owned goats, a cow, sheep, and a cat. Her relationship with them went far beyond just feeding and taking care of them. They were close to her, almost like house pets. Mom named one of the goats Barsa and loved her very much. Even when the goat was three blocks away, Mom would call, "Barsa, come here!" and the goat would come running. Meh, ah, ah, ah, Barsa would bleat as she raced eagerly towards my Mom. It was an amusing sight to watch.

"Come on! Come on!" Mom would shout happily. "I have something for you!"

When Barsa's hooves screeched to a halt before her, Mom would give Barsa a cookie. The excited goat would gobble it up with sheer delight. Dad would call Barsa too, but Barsa didn't respond to him. The goat would simply snort and turn her head away. She was probably the only living thing in Lebanon that could get away with ignoring Dad like that.

It wasn't just Barsa that loved my Mom. All the animals on the farm loved her. She knew how to nurture and build relationships with them. She possessed extraordinary attributes that allowed the animals to feel comfortable around her. The love she gave them was genuine. She didn't prize them for their milk or the money they would give her, as my Dad did. Even to this day, I don't know how to explain the connection. I have never experienced such a bond with animals in my whole life. I try to build a relationship with a cat or dog and create some semblance of what my Mom had, but it has never come close.

Mom even had a turtle friend! One day, as she was walking in the garden, she saw a turtle at her feet. Mom gave her some food and brought her some bread and grass. The turtle seemed to feel comfortable with her.

"Okay, sweetheart! You can eat it! It's okay! It's okay!" Mom said.

The turtle studied her, and then she opened her mouth and started eating the grass and bread in Mom's hand. After a few more similar interactions, they became friends. Mom continued to see the turtle almost every day.

One morning, I was sitting inside when I heard something hit the closed door. Thump! thump! thump! Pom! pom! pom!

"Mama," I called, "somebody's knocking on the door! Open the door."

"Who is it?" She thought somebody was stopping by for a visit, maybe one of our family friends or neighbors. My mother hurried to the door and opened it.

Instead of a friend or neighbor, lo and behold, there stood the turtle! It was unreal! I would not have believed it if I hadn't seen it with my own eyes.

"Guess who's here?" Mom asked, with her head stuck halfway out the door.

"Who?" I asked.

"It's the turtle."

"Nooo!" I was genuinely shocked.

She said, "Trust me, I'm not kidding!"

Mom said to the turtle, "Okay, I'm going to feed you."

The turtle was not very big. Mom went to the kitchen and brought back a piece of bread, cucumbers, and carrots. The turtle sat down, relaxed, and happily ate the food. She took her time. I couldn't believe how slowly she ate the food. I told my friends, my neighbors, and everyone I came across. Everybody laughed about it. They all loved my Mom, and we knew that even the wild animals loved her. It was amazing to witness her infectious love.

My Mom was a sweetheart. There was something extraordinary and unique about her. I don't know what it was. If you saw her, you would love her too. You wouldn't even have to know who she was. You would feel the goodness in her heart and her love. Everyone loved my Mom. The world loved her. The trees loved her. The animals loved her.

Dad

My Dad was tough on the entire family. He was very strict and rarely showed us any love. The only emotions we ever felt from my Dad were anger and disappointment. The worst thing about it was that if one of us made a mistake, we were all in trouble.

If I made Dad angry while we were planting, my brothers and sisters felt the effects of his anger too. It wasn't just for the day either. It lingered for the whole week. He would recall the mistake that happened days earlier and demand an answer, "Why did you not obey me?" Mom tried to explain to him that we were just kids and he should be easier on us, but he just smacked her as well. Left cheek! Right cheek! He slapped her around hard, but she never stopped trying to reason with him and protect us.

When we were young, we didn't know what abuse was. We just accepted that Dad always treated us this way. We didn't know any other way. More so, we didn't have a term for it. We thought it was the culture in Lebanon. We thought it was customary to hit your sons, smack your daughters, and slap your wife. As the male of the house, you had that right. But in reality, it wasn't normal. Eventually, we found out some parents in Souane were easier on their kids. It became apparent my Dad was the worst.

A typical day in our house consisted of the following: Before we went to bed, my Dad prepared us for what chores we were to do the next day. In the early morning, after we all kissed his hand, Dad would take us to the garden while Mom prepared breakfast. We helped him plant tomatoes, kidney beans, potatoes, and herbs in the fertile, brown soil. At only seven or eight years old, I began working in the garden. But I was always terrified because I was keenly aware of the harsh punishment that was awaiting me if I did something wrong. I was not very good at planting. Because of my inexperience, Dad always gave me strict instructions.

"Plant them this way," he would say.

"Yes," I replied, but I didn't understand what he said because fear blocked out my ability to think. I froze and struggled to follow his directions. I felt even more fear and anger. Other times, I thought I understood, but my lack of self-confidence and experience caused me to question myself and do the opposite. It seemed I could never get it right.

When he saw me planting in the wrong direction, his face grew as red as the tomatoes. "Didn't I tell you where to plant the tomatoes? Why aren't you listening?"

I would answer very calmly and quietly, "I don't know. I wanted to plant there instead."

Smack! Dad would spank me right then and there, with no warning, because I hadn't listened to his instructions. That made me even angrier. I was a headstrong, stubborn little girl with no power or will to fight back. Instead, I just took the beating and resolved to create more trouble for my father every chance I got. That was my way of fighting back. Not with my hands, not with my words, but with my behavior.

The best times of my childhood, the most fun times, were when Dad traveled to the city of Byblos. He was an entrepreneur and he was building apartments that he needed to supervise regularly. Mom sometimes went with him. Every so often, Dad spent a night in the city because the apartments kept him working late. Besides building apartments, Dad was a farmer. He sold fruits and vegetables from his garden and trees. He also sold milk from the cows, sheep, and goats he raised on our farm. Dad sold the fruits and vegetables in the city, and people came to the house to buy milk from my Mom.

When Dad took a trip to the city, the entire mood of the house changed. It was as if I could finally breathe without worrying if I was breathing too loudly or noisily for his taste. I got up early in the morning and put on work clothes that I wore to feed the animals. I always carried a bucket of water with me for the animals. Making sure the animals had water to drink was my job. We all had strict orders from my Dad as to what we must do, with no excuses or complaints.

During the day, I played house and other games with my girlfriends and neighbors. I often played at my girlfriend's home. We talked and used our imaginations to play games and pretend with our dolls. We always treated our prized toys with respect and took great care of them.

One of my favorite games involved a large, round rock. I would scour the ground for a suitable one. Then I would take the big rock and roll it up and down the paved street until I grew tired. I found it exhilarating and fun, not because I had any weird penchant for rocks, but because, finally, no one was telling me what to do or how to do it. I felt relaxed and satisfied that I was doing something I enjoyed without criticism. There was no right or wrong way to roll a rock. This was my game with my rules. Also, I learned that if I continued playing with the stone, in time, it would get smoother and prettier.

It wasn't only me who felt this sense of complete freedom and relief when my Dad was gone. My siblings walked with a relaxed gait and their minds were at peace. They played freely without fearing my Dad's wrath. It was like free time. We knew that when we returned home, we would not get punished. It felt good to play like young kids should play: with joy, a little mischief, and with few inhibitions. We weren't sweating about what we might have done wrong or getting threatened by my Dad for who knows what.

When my father went to the city, Mom enjoyed her time too. She smiled more when Dad wasn't around. She could breathe easier, visit the neighbors, and do all the things she wanted to do. My Mom only smoked when my Dad wasn't around. He didn't want to waste money on cigarettes. We were all happy, and our home became a happy place. We didn't have to worry about anger or violence when he was away. However, like all good things, that only lasted for a short time.

When Dad was in the house, everyone walked on eggshells because even a wrong look or small mistake could set off his temper. Upon his return home, reality set in and we would all mope around with sad faces. Even Mom looked unhappy and on edge those few hours right before he returned. Then the dreaded moment came when he arrived. When I heard the Volkswagen coming up the street, my stomach began to hurt. I listened for the loud horn of the Volkswagen go Beep! Beep! Beep! I felt like I was going to throw up. My stomach rumbled inside, and I wanted to go to the bathroom. Sometimes my whole body started to shake, and I felt like I couldn't think anymore. I feared my nasal passages would block up, and I would slowly run out of breath.

During my Dad's city trips, my brother, Fouad, often went hunting for birds and small animals. When he heard the roar of the Volkswagen, he ran like a wild person back to the house. He was supposed to be studying, not playing. Dad wanted us to work hard on our homework because education was essential to him. By the time Dad came through the door, my brother would be back in the house with his head stuck inside a schoolbook. Dad came into the house and looked at us.

"Hi Dad," I said politely.

"Hi," he replied.

One by one, we took turns greeting him. In our family, we had to kiss our father's hand when he entered the house. It was a sign of respect. We didn't ever hug, although we did sometimes give a small peck on the cheek. What we did was mostly tradition. When Dad came home in a bad mood, he didn't want a kiss on the cheek, just a kiss on the hand. If I didn't kiss his hand, he would get agitated with me.

For the most part, I followed the lead of my brothers and sisters, but sometimes I would be so angry that I would not kiss him on the hand. My refusal to kiss his hand angered him even more.

"Why didn't you kiss me on the hand?" he would ask. I didn't reply because I was angry at him. When I was angry, I didn't have any control over what I did and how I behaved. I didn't want to kiss his hand. I just wanted to do something he hated.

I stared at him and thought in my mind, "I can't stand you."

He would say, "What are you staring at?"

"Nothing," I would mumble, but in my head I thought, "I wish you weren't here. I wish you were somewhere else. I can't stand you. I don't love you. I wish you weren't my Dad. I would be happier if my

Mom married somebody else. Why can't you show us some love and treat us better?" I became so angry that I wished he were dead.

Dad kept asking, "What are you thinking? What's on your mind?" I just stared at him. "Nothing."

If I told him what I was thinking, I would probably not be here today. I knew he could not control what I was thinking. That was one thing out of his control. Most memories of my Dad are that he was always mean to us.

He was strict and didn't use good judgment in how he punished us. An example of his poor parental skills is when he sent me walking down a path leading to the family cemetery, at night, alone. My Mom pleaded with him to change his mind. She didn't think it was a good idea to send a seven year-old girl down a pitch-dark path alone. He said it was good for her to confront her fears. It was a bad idea. The fear inside of me intensified as I felt my way through bushes, in complete darkness, trying to find the path. I could hear animals rustling around me as I walked slowly. When I reached the cemetery, my fear lingered because I still had to feel my way back home. I kept asking myself, "Why am I here? What did I do to deserve this?" It was one of the scariest things I've ever experienced. If my Dad was trying to help me get over being scared, it was the wrong way. If anything, it drove fear deeper into my soul. It is something I will not forget. His intentions may have been good, but his methods were not good. I believe he treated us the way his Dad treated him when he was growing up.

One good thing about my Dad is he wanted all of us to be educated and smart. We attended expensive private schools, and we all had beautiful clothes to wear. He always reminded us to eat slowly, not to laugh loudly, and to be neat. Dad was neat and organized and insisted on us being the same. My Dad was also very punctual, and if we were late for dinner, we were not allowed to eat until the next meal. I loved to eat, so I was usually on time for every meal. My Dad used to tell me I ate like a pig. That was somewhat true because after everyone was finished eating and left the table, I would eat whatever was still on everyone's plates. That is likely why I was a little overweight, and the rest of my family was trim. He taught us that being fat wasn't good for our health.

On one occasion, my Mom and Dad were in Byblos taking care of business. They planned to be there for two days, and Dad asked the neighbors to check in on us. In the afternoon of the day they left, I started feeling hot like I had a fever. I didn't think much about it, so I didn't tell anyone. By the next morning, the day they were coming home, I was very sick and started getting a rash on my face. By the afternoon, I started bleeding from my nose. I was suffering like there was no tomorrow. My sister, Suead, gave me a bucket to catch my blood. I filled about three coffee cups full of blood. She was worried, but she knew Mom and Dad were soon to be home.

When they returned to the house, Suead cried out, "Look! Look! Something is wrong with Amira! She has a rash and is bleeding from her nose!"

Mom said, "Oh my God! What's going on here?"

She saw the rash all over my body and said, "Amira, it looks like you have chickenpox."

"I have an idea," Dad said. "She has lost a lot of blood, let her drink it back."

"Are you crazy?" Mom screamed. "You can't force her to drink her blood! You'd kill her!" The blood in the bucket was thick and dark like jello. I was only six years old, and if Mom didn't step in, I might have been forced to drink my blood! This time, Mom put her foot down. She gave him a stern look and said, "It is too dangerous for her to drink her blood! She needs to see a doctor!"

She was right. It was dangerous. I am glad he didn't make me drink it. She quickly threw the blood out. Dad drove me to the doctor with my Mom sitting next to me. The doctor gave me lots of water to drink and treated me for chickenpox.

Lentils

I continually got in trouble with Dad because I didn't follow his instructions. I purposely did the opposite of what he said most of the time. However, when I was six years old, there was another reason why I did not listen to my Dad.

It was during the evening, and my parents and I were in the kitchen. Dad was sitting at the dining table by himself.

"Amira, would you get me a spoon?" he asked. I didn't do anything because I didn't hear him.

"Amira!" he said again and turned to face me. Again, I didn't do anything.

Smack! Before I knew it, my father was towering over me. His hands were red from slapping me hard several times on the face. My mother rushed over and begged him to stop.

"Something is wrong with your daughter," he huffed, his face flushed. "It's not just about listening. Something is wrong, something mentally."

Mom looked at me and said, "What's wrong with her? She's fine." She came down to my level and said, "Amira."

I cocked my head and looked at her blankly. "Something is wrong with her," she agreed.

Both my parents leaned down to see what was going on. As they inspected me, Mom suddenly stopped when she looked into my ears. She stuck her small finger inside my ear, and lentils came falling out. Lentils are red, green, or yellow dried beans used to make soups or broths. When Mom took a closer look in my ears, she found more lentils. I had clumps and clumps of them in my ears. There were some in the right and a bunch in the left. Both ears were full.

"Look what she has in her ears," Mom murmured.

"Oh my God!" my sister, Suead, exclaimed when she saw what Mom was pulling out.

Suead, Dad, and Mom crowded around me with the tweezers and took turns trying to get the lentils out of my ears. One by one, the small lentils were carefully plucked out. When all of the lentils were removed, I suddenly felt better for the first time in a long while. I could finally hear everything going on around me. Before, I could see Dad's mouth opening and moving about, but I didn't know what he was saying. It was all because of those pesky lentils.

I told my parents later how the lentils had gotten into my ears in the first place. A few weeks earlier, I was sitting in the kitchen while Mom was cooking. There was a tray of lentils on the table, and I just grabbed them and started putting them into my ears when she wasn't looking. They were in there so long that one of them was beginning to sprout inside my ear! My hearing was much improved after all the lentils were removed. It sounded like a whole new world. The sounds I heard around me were finally crisp and clear. Of course, that didn't stop me from continuing to disobey my father's instructions on purpose!

My Free Time at the Beach

As I grew older, I learned how to avoid Dad's punishment. I looked forward to school being out for the summer. On weekends, Dad usually would be in the mountain taking care of his plants and animals, while we lived in Byblos with my mom. I felt freedom from his punishment while he was gone. He would come to the city once during the week to sell his goods.

I spent most of my free time at the beach with my girlfriends. Dad didn't approve of me wearing a bikini at the beach. In our culture, bikinis were considered indecent. So I told my mom I was going to my girlfriend's house, about 20 minutes away from us. Mom trusted me to tell her where I was going. I did go to my girlfriend's house, but just long enough to get ready to go to the beach with my girlfriends.

When I got back home in the evening, Mom asked, "Where have you been all day? Why is your face so red? It looks like you have a sunburn."

"I was out walking in the sun."

Each day that I planned to go to the beach with my girlfriends, I told her, "I'm going to visit my girlfriends." My mom's instincts told her something wasn't right about what I was telling her. She didn't find out the first few times. Something seemed unusual about my glee at visiting friends.

One day, she followed me to make sure I was being honest about where I was going. "You can go," Mom told me.

I had no clue she suspected me of lying to her. I went to the beach as we had done several times before. I loved the beach on the Mediterranean Sea, with its warm, white sand and light sea breeze. Life was good. Many people were there having fun.

As I was lying on the sand in my swimming suit, I saw a person about 100 feet away. It looked almost like a mirage. The figure was familiar...Oh God! It was my Mom!

I shrieked, "It's my Mom! What is she doing here? Holy cow, what is she doing here?"

Now she was standing over me, holding a stick. "You told me you were going to your girlfriend's house, right?"

"Right!" I agreed. "We came to the beach after we met at my girlfriend's house."

"What the hell are you doing here? Who are you anyway? Are you my daughter? Do we do this? Going to a beach with bikinis and looking at guys? Your Dad would kill you if he knew! How could you do this? How dare you?"

I was so embarrassed.

"Get up and walk in front of me now!"

I walked in front of her, and she talked all the way home.

"What if your Dad found out? You will cause trouble for both of us! You know how crazy your Dad is! He will hit both you and me, and he will punish the rest of the family!"

"You know, I want to have some fun in my life," I explained.

My Dad hadn't seen me for about ten days, and when he came back from the mountains, he immediately looked at my face and asked, "Why are you so tanned?"

"I was walking out in the sun every day."

I'm not sure why, but somehow he trusted me. I was so relieved and happy that he believed my explanation. I had to tell one lie to cover-up another one. I couldn't tell him the truth and see my Mom punished. I felt like I had no option.

"Don't go out in the sun without a hat on," he advised. I started wearing a hat the next day, hoping this would protect my Mom from Dad's wrath.

Eventually, Dad found out the real reason my skin was so tanned. He asked me why I didn't tell him the truth. I told him I was afraid he would hit me and punish Mom. I learned that lying could prevent punishment. It was the only way I could have fun and not get penalized for it.

Chapter 2
My Brothers and Sisters

There were six kids in our house: From left to right, Adnan (not shown), the oldest and best-liked by my Dad; Issam, the sweet one that Dad picked on the most; Fouad, the spoiled one; Nada, the youngest; Suead, the nice and sensitive one and me.

I don't remember much about Nada because she was much younger than me compared to my other siblings. Mostly I remember hitting her when I got upset because she wanted to follow me everywhere I went.

Issam was sincere and straightforward in any work he did at school or home. When Dad asked him to complete a task, he did it very well. Issam's work ethic was one thing Dad admired about my middle brother. He would say, "What I like about you, son, is when I give you something to do, you do your job very well. You are very organized, neat, and clean." Sometimes Issam did the job even better than Dad would. That's how meticulous and detailed he was.

Fouad was a small, blonde-haired boy. Dad was blonde too, and he liked this about my brother. Fouad's blonde hair was long and pleasant because my mother rarely cut it. Dad spoiled Fouad the most, giving him money, hugging him, and loving him. I remember I used to look at my little brother and think, "Oh, I wish I had long hair. I wish I were blonde. I wish, I want. I wish everything." Whenever he got noticed, I wished I was him.

Because of the attention he got, Fouad became very lazy and spoiled. Although he was smart, he was not good at school and was dishonest with any work he did. Dad was tougher on him as he got older. Dad used to give him work to do in the garden.

"Go water the tomatoes and beans," Dad would say.

"Okay," Fouad replied, but he would find a way to cheat. Instead of spraying the soil until it was wet, he would spray the plants, and they wouldn't appear to get enough water.

"Did you finish?" Dad asked when he came back home.

"Yes," Fouad replied.

"No, you didn't water them well! Why did you lie to me?" Boom! Boom! Boom! Dad punched him right and left.

Fouad never did a job which met my Dad's standards. When Dad gave him a responsibility or chore, he was never satisfied, not once. Dad yelled at him, punished him, and spanked him, but it didn't make a difference. Fouad always did things the same way. "This is who I am," he would say.

Because of the constant friction between them, Fouad grew up having a poor relationship with our Dad. They fought like two wild animals going at it. If they could have divorced each other, they would have. As I remember, Dad always openly displayed his disdain toward Fouad.

"If I don't see you," he told Fouad, "I'll be a healthy man. I wish you'd go somewhere else for the rest of my life."

"I wish you'd go out of my life. I'd be a healthy man too." Fouad shared the sentiment. He was the only one who talked back to my Dad. He was like a tiger!

Dad often told Fouad, "I don't understand you."

"I don't understand you," Fouad replied. "What kind of quality father are you? I don't care about you."

As a result, Dad often hit him very terribly. Fouad wanted to strike back, but he always stopped himself.

"You know what?" Fouad would say. "I don't want to put my hand on you because I'll kill you if I start."

Their relationship was like this until Dad died. Fouad refused to visit Dad when he visited us in America or to go to his funeral when he died in Lebanon. That's how bad it was between them. Dad cursed his youngest son until the day he died. He never wished him well or gave him any blessings. Dad was 83 years old when he passed away.

"I hope," Dad used to say, "God will take care of you. I hope God will give you what you deserve."

Fouad wished him the same.

The only one who got away from Dad's wrath was Adnan. He was strong, and Dad thought Adnan was the smartest and bravest one in the family. Dad got along with him because Adnan was the oldest and could give him advice. Adnan once told him, "You can make me an educated man, or I will work as a farmer. I don't want to be a farmer. I want to become educated. I want to be a teacher. I want to do this in my lifetime."

Dad listened to my brother and did what Adnan wanted to do. We all knew Adnan was very wise. When my parents were not home, Dad always left Adnan to take care of us. Adnan would study and watch us like a second father. But Adnan had a quick temper, maybe even worse than Dad. If he didn't talk, he used his fist. He was a teenager with way too much power.

When Adnan asked my brother, Issam, to study, Issam said, "No, I'll study later. Don't tell me what to do."

"Hey, hey!" Adnan said, "Remember, you have to listen to what your Dad said. And you have to listen to me."

"What are you talking about?" Issam responded.

Then, boom! Adnan hit him in the stomach, and Issam sank to the floor.

My sister, Suead, also got many smacks from Adnan. He always put her down and told her how stupid she was. All of us, equally, had poor self-esteem. I recall when Adnan wanted her to cook soup for dinner, and Suead didn't know how to cook. She was only 12 years old. When Adnan sipped on the tasteless soup, he got angry and smacked her across the room. Sometimes he kicked her. When she fell on the floor, the kicking continued. Her small body became limp with the blows from his foot. Dad did the same thing to Mom when he didn't like the food.

Adnan was a macho man. He was tough on all of us, but he took it a little easier on me. I had a girlfriend that Adnan liked, so he was kind to me. When I brought my friend to the house, Adnan would talk to her. She was a beautiful girl.

One day, Adnan told me, "If you bring your friend over, I won't hit you."

"You won't?" I asked.

"Nope," he said.

"Okay!" He treated me much better after that.

I was very close to Issam, my middle brother. I liked to follow him when he went outside. Issam wanted to go to the field, find a nest inside a tree, and catch the small chicks. He brought them home, fed them until they were a little bigger, and sold them...a baby bird for twenty-five cents. If business was slow, he would offer the bird for ten or fifteen cents.

One day, I went to the field just to have fun and do the same thing. I saw a nest, climbed the tree, and found a chick. I brought it home.

"Where did you get this?" Issam asked. I told him I found it in the field.

"If I give you a quarter, will you give it to me?"

"Yes," I said. "When will I get the quarter?"

"I'll give it to you next week," he said. "I promise."

"Okay," I shrugged and gave the chick to him.

Next week arrived, and Issam hadn't fulfilled his end of the deal.

"You didn't give me a quarter yet!" I said.

"Well, I don't have it," Issam told me. "When I have it, you'll get it."

"Okay," I said. I waited for almost three weeks, and I still didn't see my quarter. What should I do,? I thought to myself. I was about ten years old at the time.

Soon thereafter, I watched him when he collected money from people. He had a place where he secretly stored all his money, and I wanted to find that place. He always closed the kitchen door when he hid his money, but he forgot this time. I saw him put money into a big jar. Oh, I see the money, I thought, as he added money into it. The moment I got a chance, I went directly to that jar, opened it, and took a quarter. When Issam came back that evening after selling more birds, he counted his money and immediately noticed one quarter was missing. He went crazy!

I thought to myself, "Oh-oh, I'm going to be a dead person!" and I gulped and did the only thing I knew. I ran!

Issam cried because someone took his money. My other brother said, "Why are you crying?"

"My quarter! Somebody took my quarter! Somebody took my quarter!" Issam cried and ran off.

Adnan asked me, "Did you take his money?"

"Yes," I replied. "I took it. But my brother didn't give me the quarter he promised me."

I also told my Mom the truth when she asked about it. "Did you do it?" she asked.

"Yes."

"Why did you do that?"

I said, "Mama, he did not give me the quarter he owed me! He lied to me! That's why I took it." She told Issam, "Amira is the one. She took your quarter."

Holy cow! He jumped at me! I sank, and Mom went between us.

"Hold on! Hold on!" Mom said, grabbing Issam, "Wait a minute! Wait a minute! I'm the mama. What are you doing to your sister?"

Issam shouted, "She took my money!" He was swearing. He was so mad at me. "She's stupid! She took my money!"

"Why did you do this to her? Why didn't you pay her as you promised?" Mom demanded. Issam could not answer Mom's questions.

From that day on, Issam did not want to get along with me. But I still followed him because I knew he was going to find more nests.

One day, he was walking when he saw me behind him. He stopped. "Are you following me?"

"Yes."

"What do you want from me?" he asked, frustrated.

"I don't want anything from you," I replied. But truthfully, I wanted to find a bird and take it.

"Wherever I go, you follow me! I can't stand you! I hate you!" Issam yelled.

Without warning, he picked up a big, heavy stone and threw it at me. It came towards my face, on the left side. Pow!

"Okay," I said calmly, "when Dad comes home, I'm going to tell him about this."

"Go to hell!" Issam screamed. "Tell him!"

Later that day, I told my Dad what happened.

Dad called to Issam, "Come here! Why did you hit her?"

"Dad!" Issam protested. "She wanted to take my bird. She always follows me wherever I go."

"Go give her a hug," Dad said, "Give her a kiss, and ask her to forgive you."

"Forgive me? No!" Issam said.

"I'm telling you," Dad said sternly. "Do it now."

Issam looked at me and mumbled, "Forgive me."

I could tell he didn't mean it. His words were hollow. "It's okay," I shrugged.

Whenever we got mad at each other, Dad insisted, "Go and ask for forgiveness. Ask for forgiveness because you made a mistake." If I was angry with my brother, Dad would say, "Go to your brother and tell him you forgive him. Kiss him." Before we went to bed, we kissed each other or asked for forgiveness. It was essential to Dad because his family hit each other from a very young age. So Issam and I made up in front of Dad.

Everything was fine until I almost drowned in the pool.

Dad had built a pool on the second story of our house. It was a small pool, about 5' square and 2' deep, with tiny, colorful fish in it. One day, Issam asked me, "You want to ride piggyback?" "Yes!" I replied, and he lifted me onto his back.

Issam carried me around for a while, and I was so happy. I screamed with delight as I clung to his shoulders. Then he set me down on the edge of the pool. As he walked away, I slipped off the side of the pool and into the water, face first.

When my face hit the water, I screamed, "Oh my God!" I couldn't breathe underwater. I was so panicked because I thought I was going to die. The water bubbled around me and roared Boom! Boom! Boom! Boom!

"Whooowwwoooch!" I screamed as I gasped for air. I felt there were seconds separating me from drowning.

Suead heard the sounds coming from the water, the splashing, and the screaming. She ran! As she pulled me from the pool, I tried to breathe. I had swallowed a large amount of water.

Suead looked at me and then stared at Issam. "What did you do to your sister?" she asked.

"I don't know," Issam answered. "It just happened."

Before she could prod further, he said, "No, I didn't do it on purpose! I didn't do it on purpose! She just fell in."

When I could finally breathe normal, I mumbled, "I don't think he wanted to kill me. Not really. He was playing."

After that, the fear of water stayed with me for a long time, and I always wondered what would have happened if Suead had not saved me. I know my brother didn't mean to hurt me. Issam had a sweet heart. But when he was angry, you had better be far away from his sight. Issam was the kind of guy who smacked whatever was around him when he was aggravated. He still has a temper today, but he's changed a lot since we were kids, and I love him dearly today.

Chapter 3
Grandma

My grandma, Dad's mom, lived with us. She wasn't the typical, loving grandmother who baked cookies and cared for us when we were sick or hurt. Unfortunately, my grandma was a nasty woman, God rest her soul.

She always chased me around our house in Lebanon. It had a flat roof, unlike most homes in the United States. I was a little wild when I was seven years old, and I liked to run along the edge of our flat roof. It was a two-story house, so if I fell, I would likely be dead instantly. The ground beneath me was cold, hard cement. If I even grazed the pavement, that would be the end of me. Still, I did it because I had so much energy as a child. When I ran on the roof, my grandma would squint and look up to see me.

"Oh my God, oh my God, oh my God!!" she shouted. "You're going to fall! I hope you will! It will teach you a lesson!"

That was the kind of woman she was. She would say, "You're going to fall! What are you doing? Are you crazy? Are you crazy?" She was always watching me and telling me don't do this or don't do that! "I hope you fall! I hope you fall because you are a bad girl! I hope you fall!" my grandma screamed. I wanted to make her upset. It was kind of like how I planted seeds in the opposite direction that Dad instructed just to make him mad.

While she was telling me this, I thought, whatever makes her angry, I'm going to do it. Even if I fall, even if I die, I want to do it to make her angry. It would be worth it. That's how I was. I would have sacrificed my own life just to make her mad. It was my way of rebelling against the way she treated me.

My grandma was not nice or kind to any of us except Issam, the one who got punished the most from my Dad. The only person she loved was Issam, and I was the one she hated the most. To the rest, my grandma was barely okay. By "okay," I would give her a low D-. She was not the type of person who protected us when we were in trouble with Dad. Instead, she added more problems.

The most prevalent memory of my grandma is when she would tell me, "You are a dummy! I'm going to tell your Dad about you. You are no good!"

Then, as soon as she saw Dad, she would tell him, "Amira's stubborn! She has a big head! You need to punish her!"

Boom! Dad would hit me. She always made things worse.

You know when you have a bad day, you come to your grandma, and she says, "It's okay, honey, I love you." She kisses you, hugs you, and makes you feel better? We didn't have that.

Dad insisted we treat Grandma with the utmost respect. He used to tell me, "When you talk back to Grandma, or answer back to her in a bad way, you will be in big trouble. You must show respect to your Grandma. I respect your Grandma because she is my mom. You must respect her as well."

"Yes," I nodded, without sincerity, because I didn't respect her.

Dad continued to warn us, "Grandma is going to write down your name if you give her a hard time while I am gone. And when I return, if there is one name on her list, you will all be in deep trouble. Am I making myself clear? Do you understand what I am telling you?" I said, "Yes, I understand." Dad always kissed her hand, just like he insisted we do for him, when he returned home.

But Grandma was such an unpleasant lady, and I did not like her at all. There was nothing to like about her. She did not have a heart, and if she did, she never showed it. Whenever she was with my Dad, she put more fire in his pan and sparked his anger even more. I remember she used to cause my Mom much trouble.

One day, when I was very young, Dad came home with oranges he had bought while in the city. Oranges were very expensive, so it was like a treat. Mom, Grandma, and Dad were all in the kitchen. Grandma said she wanted to give my mother an orange.

Mom shook her head, "No, I don't want an orange. I'm not in the mood to eat an orange." Grandma acted surprised. "You don't want to take it from me? What's wrong? Are you mad at me?"

My mom looked at her, not allowing her reaction to appear on her face. Mom said calmly, "No, Ma, I don't want an orange."

Grandma ignored her. Dad spoke up and told Mom to take the orange because it was good for her. He said, "Okay, Zeinab (my mom), take it from her."

"I don't want it," Mom repeated patiently.

Dad looked at her with glaring eyes. There was a chalkboard nearby. We wrote on the chalkboard to practice our grammar and math. In a split second, Dad grabbed the chalkboard from the wall and hurled it at my mom. Mom ducked quickly to avoid it, yelling "Ouch!" as she dove to her right. The chalkboard flew a few centimeters past her head and crashed onto the floor.

Grandma looked at my mom, then at my Dad. "Ohhh, son, why did you do that?" she whined. There appeared to be just the slightest glimmer of satisfaction in her eyes. She intentionally caused problems to get a reaction out of my Dad. He was always at the brink of exploding. Instead of cooling off the issue, she added fuel to the fire.

Dad screamed at my Mom, "You're a dummy! I'm your husband! If I tell you to do something, you do it! Even if you don't want the orange, take it!" He was swearing. "What's wrong with you?" You would think my Mom would shrink and cry by now, but she was stubborn as well. "No, I don't want it," she said quietly. Mom didn't care about her life anymore. She refused to eat the orange.

Finally, Grandma said, "Oh, please son, stop, stop!" and Dad stopped his rant and walked away. Mom looked at Grandma with great disdain. She could not openly scold her and ask, "Why did you do that to me?" Otherwise, she would be in even worse trouble with my Dad.

My grandma's presence in our home was very unpleasant to my mom, my sisters, and me. When she died, I was at peace. I felt alright and didn't even cry. It wasn't a big deal to me because she was not a good grandma to us. She's gone, I thought. I don't have to worry about her anymore. I was 14 years old when she died.

Oddly enough, I dreamed about Grandma many times after her death. I saw her often because she wouldn't let me go. In my dreams, when I got in trouble, she would come to me and talk. When I was not feeling well, she would appear and cover me with a white sheet. When I went to bed sad, because of my Dad, my environment, my life, she was there to comfort me. She didn't want me to stay sad.

Grandma was much better to me in my dreams than she was in reality. She was the Grandma I always wanted. Maybe she appeared so often because she felt guilty, I am not sure. My grandma died at the age of 65. I saw her in my dreams for the very last time around ten years ago. Her kindness in my dreams made my memories of her less painful. It is sad that I only had a loving Grandma in my thoughts after she passed away.

Chapter 4
Feeding the Sheep

When I was a little girl, one of my household chores was to feed the animals on the farm. It was an essential job because Dad prized those animals even more than his children. After all, they gave him milk, food, and money, while we were just more mouths to feed.

One morning, Dad came to me, his face stern and unsmiling. "I'm going to the city today. Make sure you feed the animals. I will be back in three days."

Before he left, Dad looked at me one more time. His voice was calm but cold. "If I find out the sheep were hungry or did not have enough water, you're in trouble." With my father, one of the best things you could tell him, one that would keep you out of harm's way, was "Yes, Dad."

I hurried to do what Dad ordered so I could play and enjoy myself afterward. I took the sheep to the field where they usually ate. After walking the sheep back to the house, I filled a bucket of water so they could drink.

"Drink," I commanded.

One of the sheep just stared at me with its beady, black eyes and refused to budge.

"Drink!" I said more sternly, in a voice that echoed my father's.

She cocked her head to the right, and then turned away and appeared bored. My anger had been slowly bubbling to a boiling point. If my father came home and found out his precious sheep had not drank water, I would be in big trouble.

"You're a son of a gun!" I finally exploded after a third attempt. "You don't want to drink water? You're going to get me in trouble!"

Without thinking, my leg flew out, and I kicked the sheep directly on the soft underside of her stomach. I kicked her hard because I was afraid of being punished when my Dad returned. I could already imagine the swift smack of my father's hands against my face. "Don't get me in trouble!" I said, angrily. "You have to drink water before my Dad comes." Again, I kicked her in the stomach.

Suddenly, her delicate body slid down to the ground. In a matter of seconds, she was lying flat, her body unmoving and her face expressionless. Oh my God! This sheep that my Dad had entrusted in my care, this sheep that he treasured, was dead, gone! This meant that when Dad came home and found her dead, I wouldn't be around anymore either. Maybe I would go to heaven, or perhaps I would go to hell because I had killed the sheep. I looked at the dead sheep one last time, but there was nothing to be done. She was in another place now.

I went back to the house, and the first thing I did was look for a piece of paper. I knew I was going to get a massive blow when Dad came home, so I wanted to soften the blow. With a pencil between my shaking fingers, I started writing:

"Dear Dad, I miss you so much. Dad, I haven't seen you for two days. I miss you so much. I wish you were here. When you come home, I want to give you a big hug. I have something to tell you. I don't think you will be happy, but you have to forgive me. I didn't do anything wrong. The sheep died, and I have no idea why. But I want you to know. Don't be surprised. I hope you come home soon and I will explain it to you." Love, Amira

The entire letter was all about love, how I missed my father so much and wanted to see him soon. Of course, he was the last person I wanted to see, but I tried to calm him down before he came home because I had killed the sheep. I then gave the letter to a taxi driver in the village who drove peoples' messages to the city.

"Najie, give this to my Dad," pressing the letter into his hand.

"Okay," Najie looked down at me. "Why, honey?"

"I don't know," I said. "Just give him the letter."

I knew exactly why though. If Dad came home and saw the dead sheep on the ground, I would be right next to her in a matter of seconds. So I wrote the letter and gave it to Najie. What I didn't expect was that Dad would come home the same day I wrote the letter.

"Oh my God," I screamed inside my head. My body was already trembling. I'm going to be dead, next to the sheep.

When the Volkswagen came down the road, I stared at my hands and swallowed hard. Dad walked into the house and looked at me.

I looked back and said, "Hi, Dad."

He didn't say or do anything. He just stared. Finally, he told me to come with him. I had left the dead sheep in the shed on the floor of the shed, next to the chicken coop. Dad led me straight to her. When we were inside the shed, I saw the sheep lying there like a limp rag. Dad continued to hold my hand firmly. Then he looked at me very calmly. I had never seen him so calm in my life. He bent down, came directly to my eye level, and said quietly, "Tell me how the sheep died."

"Dad, I don't know. I fed her and gave her water. I came here and saw her, and she was dead. She was gone."

"Is this what happened?" he said in a tone that was not scary or threatening.

"Yes," my voice did not waver.

He stared at me for a few seconds. "Okay."

Then he didn't say anything. He didn't hurt or beat me. He didn't do anything. It was almost unbelievable.

Dad called some men to take the sheep and bury her away from the house. The whole time, Dad just looked at me. "Be careful next time. I want to find out what happened to her."

A few weeks later, Dad went to the city again. He asked me to do the same job with the other sheep, and I said I would. And then I did the same thing. I kicked the sheep in the stomach because she didn't drink the water either. I knew I was going to be in trouble, but my rage was at such a high that I couldn't control it. I kicked her again. Just like before, this sheep keeled over dead too.

When Dad came home, I told him the same story. I didn't bother writing a letter this time because I knew I had guaranteed a place for myself in the ground next to the second sheep. I prepared myself to be gone this time, but once again, Dad came home, listened to my story, and did not hit me. I was so confused. The only explanation was there must have been an angel hovering over me that told him, "Leave her alone."

Chapter 5
A House of Dummies

Our house in the mountain was on the main road going through the small village of Souane. Dad decided that the garage, located next to our house, would make an ideal location to have a store. It was facing the road and had space next to it where a customer could safely park. There was just enough extra room in his garage for him to build small shelves next to where he parked his Volkswagen. Here, people passing by could see the fruits and vegetables, candies, gum, pastries, and other items that Dad had picked up while he was in the city. We were all excited about the store and were anxious to help sell things. I worried because I envisioned myself eating the candies when it was my turn to watch the store.

On most days, Dad left my older sister, Suead, in charge of the store. Suead sold most of the items for a nickel, but because she was so young, some people walked by and stole things from the shelf. They were much older and bigger than her, so she could not stop them.

Dad always kept track of his inventory at the end of each day. He checked to see if the store's inventory matched up with the cash in the drawer. If something was missing, he became enraged. "Something is missing, and there is no money to show for it! Where's the money?" he screamed.

"I don't know," Suead shrugged timidly.

She was only 12 years old, but she knew better than to admit that people had taken the items while she helplessly watched. He might not want her to be in charge anymore.

Then Dad would erupt. "You are the dumbest girl in the world! What is wrong with you? Do you not even know how to count money? Why do I even send you to school?" He slapped her right and left with his rough hands. Suead shrunk under the force of the hits. "You're not worth anything in life! You all have a brain that God gave you, but none of you are using it. All of my kids are dummies!

You're all dummies because your mom is a dummy!" On and on, he would hurl insults at my timid sister.

The funny thing is because he told us we were dummies so often, we believed him. We began to think that our mom was a dummy. He said it all the time, so it must be true.

Ironically, the only living things in our home that Dad didn't consider dummies were the animals. He so loved the cows and goats because they gave him milk. My Dad received a direct benefit from owning them because he could sell the milk and the goats to make money. They were his treasures.

"Oh, you're so sweet," Dad would coo to the goat and give her a little pat on the head. "You're so sweet!"

I used to look at the two of them and think, "I wish I was a goat. Then maybe he would not hit me. Perhaps he would treat me as well as he treated the animals." I used to be so jealous of those animals.

One day, Suead was minding the store, and I was sitting on a little rock next to the garage. We were waiting for customers. It was her job to watch the store, and I was just hanging around. Dad came to me, with Ablah following behind him. He asked me to take Ablah, one of his prized sheep, to the property near our family cemetery. There was a lot of fresh grass near the cemetery for Ablah to eat. Dad tied one end of a rope loosely around the sheep's neck and put the other end in my hand. He tied the rope to the sheep's neck like you put a leash on a dog. It was the same rope he used to hit my mother. Of course, I said yes. There was no option to disobey him. "Put her near the cemetery where there is enough grass for her to eat."

Obediently I walked toward the cemetery with the rope in my hand. Ablah followed closely behind. Once we got there, I tied the sheep to a fence to make sure she would not wander away. I made a small, tight knot that would give Ablah about ten feet to walk. Then I went home.

When Dad saw me, he asked, "Did you put her where I told you?"

"Yes," I nodded.

"Okay, good," he said. I then went back to the store to spend time with Suead.

About an hour later, my Dad heard the sheep scream "Baaaaaaaaah! Baaaaaaaaah!" The sheep shrieked again and again.

Sensing something was wrong, Dad ran toward the sheep. He found Ablah hanging down over the fence. He observed that the rope had tightened around her slender neck as she tried to free herself. Now she was making a shrill, choking sound. "Cuhhhh," Ablah bleated, as if she was dying.

She had jumped over the fence and choked herself. The rope was barely ten feet, so when she jumped, the rope was too short, and it left her dangling over the fence. Dad grabbed the sheep and picked her up over the fence and quickly saved her life. He led Ablah to a safer area near the cemetery so she wouldn't get tangled around the fence. He tied the rope securely around a tree.

When Dad came back toward the garage, I could feel something in the air. There was a deadly calmness to him, and it terrified me. Slowly, he walked toward me, his face showing no emotions. He had a rope in his hand. Dad walked up to me and looked straight into my eyes.

I knew with certainty what was wrong with him. "I want to do to you what you did to the sheep," Dad said.

"Do what?" I asked, confused.

"I want to choke you." There was no humor in his tone. He was deadly serious.

"Choke me?" I squeaked. "Why?" I gulped as I saw the rope come closer towards my neck. Then I realized he thought it was my fault, and he wanted to teach me a lesson. He believed in an eye for an eye, or in this case, a neck for a neck.

"I want to choke you like you choked the sheep," Dad said again.

"What did I do?" I still didn't completely understand what he was talking about, but I knew enough about my father to know he didn't make empty threats. So I cupped my hands together and held them tightly under my chin to protect my neck and did the only thing that I could do. I screamed.

"Aaaaahhhhh!" I yelled as hard as I could because I knew right then that I was screaming for my life. I honestly thought I would end up buried in the family cemetery, next to where I tied up the sheep.

Dad grabbed my hands and pulled me towards him. He repeated, "I want to do to you what you did to the sheep!"

For a moment, we struggled. I fought back with all my might to protect my neck. Somehow, my will to survive was stronger than his desire to hurt me. I didn't let him do it. I got my strength by thinking of dying at my Dad's hands. Dad looked at me like, "God damn it; she's a strong girl." Then he let me go and just glared.

"Do you know what you did?" he said.

I didn't look at him because his face became so stiff and scary when he got this angry. Looking back, I don't think he wanted to kill me. He wanted to scare me and give me a lesson that I would remember for the rest of my life.

"Do you know what you did?" Dad yelled. "Only dummy people like you would put the sheep near the fence! Didn't you know it could jump the fence and hang down? It could have killed her!"

The truth is, I didn't know. I was just six years old. I never forgot that day, and I don't know if my sister forgot or not. She was near me when it started, but I don't remember where she was by the end of the whole thing. Maybe she was hiding somewhere. I don't know.

Whenever Dad had problems with one of us, he yelled at everybody. If I did something wrong, he would hit me and proceed to punish all of us. I wasn't able to do it that day, but usually I ran away when he got angry. I would run somewhere in the field and not come home for a few hours until his rage had cooled down. I could hear my Dad calling to me but I was too scared to answer.

Eventually I mustered enough courage to return. Dad would look at me and ask, "Where have you been?"

Avoiding his eyes, I replied, "I was outside." I gave him an excuse like I was watering the garden. I always came up with something.

He swore, spitting out terrible words. "It's your dummy mother's fault!" he yelled. He continued to bellow more bad words. As they came out of his mouth, they floated around and just hung there for hours. You could still feel them long after his tirade had ended.

Finally, Dad said, "Okay, go inside and study."

"Okay," I scrambled past him.

You could see on his face that he was exhausted physically and emotionally. He finished his rant. The whole day he had been yelling, hitting, and cursing at my family. It took everything out of him, leaving him weak and unable to continue his rage. Yet somehow, the cycle always continued.

Dad also didn't like the way I ate. For some reason, I ate too fast. He would always say, "Eat your food slowly. Take your time and digest your food. Eating slower is good for your stomach." He would also tell me I was eating too much, that I needed to eat about half. Looking back, maybe he was right because I was getting a little chubby.

He would ask me, "Do you understand why I want you to eat slowly?"

I said, "Yes," but actually I didn't hear or understand anything he said. I just ate fast. I liked to finish quickly.

He looked at me and said, "What did I say?"

So I ate slowly for the rest of my meal. Eating fast was normal for me, though. When I would get up from the dinner table, Dad would say, "You ate too fast and too much!"

My Mom also said I should slow down when I ate because I was already overweight. I used to talk fast also, and he'd say, "Slow down." Everybody told me I talked too quickly and too loudly.

Dad didn't like my laugh either. My laugh was unrestrained and uncontrolled. He said when I laughed, I didn't look sophisticated or educated. He said I needed to smile like a lady and not laugh so loud.

"That's why I don't want you to laugh too loud. It's not good for girls to laugh too loud."

I didn't understand what he was saying. Laughing came naturally to me. When I found something to be funny, I let it out.

Thinking back, the only thing Dad liked about me was the fact that I was a good dancer. Other than dancing, though, he made me feel worthless. I always felt demoralized. He did not treat me with respect. He didn't even like the way I stood up. I would stand up straight as he instructed, and he'd say, "Put your shoulders back and straighten out." I was very depressed. I always looked like I was slouching. I felt like I couldn't do anything to please my Dad. I tried to desperately keep my back straight and do all of the things he ordered me to do.

During this period in my life, I was beginning my highway to maturity, my road to personal growth. Pain, suffering, and anger already riddled my life. I had to crawl instead of move along with other kids who could run. I even crawled on the highway as a child. Each fear, each angry outburst from my Dad, each terrifying moment that I questioned my survival still influences my struggle to be successful in life. I experience insecurities and fears of being wrong about something I know very well. It takes me longer to gain confidence in myself.

Someone who grew up with positive experiences can run through life with self-confidence and a positive attitude. I had to struggle and crawl through all of this and still move forward. But I didn't get off my highway, despite how rough the road became. If I wanted to live, I had to keep moving forward. Whatever my Dad did to me made my road almost impassable. Regardless, I kept going. I didn't know whether he was going to hit me in the head. I didn't know when he was going to snap. I didn't even know where I was going, but I knew I had to keep crawling, and maybe, someday, I would be able to fly.

Chapter 6
Education in Lebanon

Education was essential in our family. Besides his farm duties and building apartments, Dad worked as a handyman in the local school, fixing leaks and broken appliances or anything else that a maintenance man would do. The faculty and administration soon realized he was a brilliant man and hired him as a substitute teacher. From that point on, he had two jobs at the school: handyman and school teacher.

I was five years old at the time. I used to go to school with my Dad and sister. Dad was excellent at numbers and math. He used to ask his students what two plus two was. Then he would look at me and ask the same question. I tried hard to think of the correct answer, but I was always wrong.

"How could you give me the wrong answer?" he asked angrily. I couldn't say anything because I was not good at math. "Come here," he told me.

He spanked me hard in front of the other students. Sometimes he held me by my ears with both hands so my legs dangled above the floor. Then in one swift motion, he dropped my body to the floor.

Dad expected us to be smart. He put fear in our heads. When he glared at me, I couldn't think. I knew he was about to punish me. I knew I was going to be in trouble. So when he would say, "Think about it," after asking me a question, I had no time to think. All I could think about was that he was going to hurt me. As a result, fear grew in my heart. He continued to test me and asked more math questions.

"If I brought one chicken up here, and if I brought one goat, and then a cow, in the same room, how many are there altogether?"

Dear God, I thought. My mind was already in a state of panic. I kept thinking, one cow, one goat, and a chicken? I had no idea. I would get confused with the three things mixed.

"Four," I tried to sound confident.

"I cannot believe what..." he started to say. Then, whatever was near him, a book or a pencil, he threw it at me.

I ducked to avoid the oncoming object. I was much better at dodging flying books than answering simple math problems.

"You're not smart! You're a dummy! You're a dummy!" Dad would spit in my face. I tried to wipe it off my face with my bare hands. He then screamed, "You are like an animal! You're no different than an animal!"

I believed I was a stupid little animal girl. From an early age, Dad told me I was not worth much in this life. "If you are hungry," he would snarl, "It's not even worth it for you to eat. You're a dummy. I would give your food to the animals rather than you. At least it would do them good and not be wasted on a dummy." My Dad never passed up a chance to remind me how stupid I was.

My self-esteem dipped to zero at a very young age. All I could feel was low self-worth and fear of never becoming smart like other kids. When he talked to me, I avoided looking at his face and stared at his hands. When he asked me questions, I couldn't even hear him. My brain started to lock up, and all I could see was his tanned, muscular hands. That image is one I remember well.

What he did achieve was instill a fear of learning, a fear of being wrong. I wanted to get the right answers because I wanted so much to be smart and do well in school. I also wanted to understand the lesson because I didn't want to be hurt anymore. Unfortunately, I was ill-prepared to face the beginning of my formal education.

Public School

When I was six years old, Dad always drove me to school. It was a public school located in the mountain, and Dad taught kindergarten there. I had a different teacher, of course, but Dad was in the next room, teaching his small group of students.

One day, my teacher was teaching us grammar. He looked around the room, asking everybody questions. When he looked at me, he asked me to read. Oh no, I thought. I am not a good reader. I struggled through the words and made many mistakes as I read aloud. When I finished, I looked up at him. It was apparent he didn't like the way I read.

"Come here," the teacher said to me in a stern voice.

"No," I replied.

In Lebanon, you cannot say "no" to the teacher. If the teacher says, "Come here," you don't walk...you run. The teacher is like a master, and you are supposed to treat him or her with the utmost respect. Me? I said, "No!"

"What?" he asked.

"No," I repeated, "I don't want to come."

I didn't go to him, so he came to me. In those days, the teachers punished students with a huge stick. They would ask you to open your hand, and then they hit you. That's what my teacher wanted to do. He had a ruler in his hand, and he came towards me. I was afraid of being hit.

"Open your hand."

"No!" I said.

"I'm asking you to open your hand," he demanded in a very stern voice.

Again, I said, "No."

He stared at me. He didn't expect to hear what I said. With a swift, rough motion, he opened my hand to hit me. I grabbed his hand and bit as hard as I could! He started screaming, and a small commotion began in our room. All the students started speaking at once, "Oh my God, look what happened! Look what she did! She bit the teacher!"

It was awful, but I knew why I did it. He didn't give me the respect that I needed, so I didn't give him respect back. The teacher wanted to hit me, and I wanted to stop him. I almost took out a piece of his hand. There were deep teeth marks where I bit down. Immediately, he stormed to the next room and told my Dad what happened. When Dad came into our room, the teacher glared and said, "Look what your daughter did! She bit me here!" He extended his hand to show Dad the deep, red impression of the full set of my teeth.

Dad exploded. "How did you do this? How dare you?" He was furious. Right then and there, he punished me. He lifted me off the floor by my ears and dropped me down on the floor, hard. He was embarrassed about what I did." How can you do this? You have to listen! You can't say no to a teacher!" From that day on, I learned to think twice before I ever said no to a teacher when Dad was around.

I learned one essential thing about myself in kindergarten. It all started one day while my teacher was giving a lesson. You know how you sit in class when you're a kid and try to avoid eye contact with the teacher, so he doesn't call on you? That was me. We had about 20 students in my class. He never called our names in order. It was always random. Sometimes he would pick a student from the front, and sometimes he would choose a student from the edges of the room.

While he was speaking, I felt like he was ready to choose me. I leaned over and told my girlfriend, "Guess what?"

"What?"

I said, "The teacher's going to call my name... right now."

"What?" she asked again. She looked confused.

"Amira," the teacher's voice boomed. "It's your turn." He called on me to read whatever we were studying that day, Arabic or grammar.

When he moved on from me, my friend just looked at me. "How did you know he was going to call your name?"

I shrugged. I just felt it. After we finished reading the next assignment, I told my friend, "Now he's going to call Ali."

Guess what? The teacher called Ali next.

"How did you know?" she asked again, with confusion. Some of my friends sitting next to me heard what I predicted and became afraid of me.

"What the heck!" my girlfriend said, as my predictions kept coming true. "How do you know? How do you know?" She was getting scared too. Then, as the lesson went on, a friend told a friend, who told another friend, until finally, the whole class was whispering about it. My teacher didn't appreciate the added noise. "Hey! Stop! What's going on? What's wrong? Hey, hey! You guys talking, stop! Stop!"

All of the students talked about me, and I was the center of attention for a while. I quickly realized predicting things like that scared the kids around me, so I stopped. I still knew who the teacher would call next, but I kept it to myself. Even to this day, I remember the strange, inexplicable sensation that would come over me right before my teacher called on someone. Little did I know back then that those small predictions would grow into something much more profound when I grew older.

I felt different from the others for some reason but didn't know why. Something inside me did not feel ordinary because no one else seemed to have the same sense that I did.

My Dad spent much of his time in the city of Byblos managing the construction of an apartment building. It was a big project that took several years to complete.

I was 8 years old when Dad finished the beautiful, large apartments. I was excited to stay in Byblos in the winter months and move to our mountain home in Souane in the summer. It was too dangerous to drive in the mountains when snow covered the narrow, winding roads during the winter months.

When my family moved to the city, I stopped going to school in the mountain. Dad enrolled my two sisters and me in a public school. We then moved out from the Byblos apartments because Dad was having a fight with his sister, Naham, over property rights issues. Dad had two sisters, Jamile and Naham. His older brother, Mouneef, died in a car accident, and his younger brother, Abid Kareem, died of cancer.

"This is yours. "No, this is mine..." "You told me I could have half of it..."

"Yes, I'll give back the money you loaned me..."

They bickered like that, back and forth. My aunt had given Dad a lump sum of money to buy half of the property, but Dad wanted more. He told her she did not give him enough money for half, so the property belonged to him. My Dad was very greedy in that way. It put a real strain on their relationship. They finally resolved their issues, and Dad paid her back for her investment. Dad said, "Well, the best thing we can do is move from this area." Dad rented out all of the apartments, and we moved.

The area we moved to was a Christian neighborhood. It was apartment living, much different than living in the house in the mountain, where we had a garden and farm animals. My sisters and I attended public school while Adnan, Issam, and Fouad attended private school.

After completing four years of public school, Adnan convinced my Dad to enroll my sisters and me in a Catholic school. It was expensive, but Adnan believed we would learn more in a private school which insisted on strict discipline. My Dad thought it would be good for us too, but it was a lot of money, and he struggled with the idea of spending too much money. It's not that Dad didn't have enough money; he was just selfish with it, even when it came to his kids. Somehow, Adnan convinced him to make a move, and enrolled Suead, Nada, and me in a private school in the city. It was a little unusual, as there were very few Muslim children enrolled in a Catholic school. After a period of time, we adjusted to the new environment. I was 14 years old.

Private School

In private school, teachers were very strict. I didn't do well with my schoolwork, with one exception. When I liked the teacher, I excelled. If I disliked my teacher, I wanted to be anywhere else but in her classroom.

"Can I go to the bathroom?" I used to raise my hand and ask.

"Sure," the teacher replied.

I walked out of the class, went to the bathroom, and just stayed there. Looking back, I realize I missed a lot of my education by sitting in the bathroom. You can't learn anything by hiding from your training. But at least I wasn't in class being intimidated or scolded. I knew I was missing out on my education, but I think I was in survival mode. It was better than taking my anger out on a teacher that I didn't like. Dad never found out about it, and the teacher didn't pay attention to it, so I got away with it.

At the same time, I brought a great deal of attention upon myself because of my dancing. I went to sporting events, and during halftime, I danced in front of the whole school.

"Wow… Wow!" Everybody fawned over me. The kids loved it, and the principal of the school was very proud to have me as a student there.

Other schools would ask, "Can we have that girl dance for us?" The answer was always, "No!" I was their girl, and other schools couldn't have me. If they wanted to see me dance, they had to come to our school to see me. The special treatment I received made me feel happy, but, mostly, it spoiled me. Because of this unique niche I had carved out for myself, I hardly studied. I thought I could get away with anything.

In private school, I quickly learned that you needed to follow all of the rules. There was a specific uniform to wear. Hair up, black shoes, and a white ribbon with a cute bow were the rules. No makeup, no long nails. If your hair was down when you arrived, the administration would send you back home to fix it. I followed all the rules for a while.

The uniform was nice. At first, I was excited to wear it. It fit well and was comfortable. However, as time went on, I grew tired of it. I was the type of person who did what I wanted to do when I didn't like something, a trait I probably picked up from my Dad. When I didn't want to wear the uniform anymore, I just didn't wear it that day.

The "Mamere" was the principal at this private Catholic school. She was the highest authority in the school. If you saw her walking in the halls, you had to bend down, get on your knee, kiss her hand, and kiss the cross she wore around her neck. If a teacher complained about you and you had to go to the Mamere, there was no mercy. They kicked you out of school. That's how strict it was.

One day, I was outside playing during a 20-minute recess when I saw the Mamere. She was wearing a loose black dress and hood. I think they call it a habit in the United States, similar to what nuns wear. I was playing when the Mamere's eyes focused on me.

"Come here, come here." Again, she repeated, "Come here!" she waved me over to where she was standing.

When the Mamere says, "Come here," you don't walk, you run. Some kids even peed in their pants. That's how respected she was. You reply, "Yes, Mamere," and immediately get on your knees.

"Yes," I walked to her.

"Where's your uniform?" the Mamere looked down at me and asked, "Why are you not wearing your uniform?"

"Because I don't want to," I retorted.

"What?"

"I don't want to," I said even stronger.

"Why?"

"I don't feel like wearing it."

"You must be kidding! You must be kidding me!"

"No," I shrugged. "I don't want to wear it."

"Go on your knees right now," she ordered crossly. "Go down on your knees," she repeated.

"No!" I said.

"No?" she said with a look of disbelief.

With a touch of exasperation, she quickly raised her head high, turned, and stormed away as she muttered, "I'm not going to be bothered with you."

Just like that, she let me go. I was shocked. Whenever the Mamere saw a student not wearing their uniform, she ordered them, "Down, down, down, down! Go on your knees, go on your knees!" There were many students who forgot to wear their uniforms. One by one, students would go on their knees. She punished everyone by making them stay on their knees for up to 20 minutes. No one dared argue with her. I was the only one. I didn't follow what she said, and when I disobeyed, she didn't punish me. I don't know why.

Maybe she thought I was too strong, and punishment would only make me even more determined. Before she left, she told me, "You will come back wearing your uniform tomorrow." I told her okay. She let me go, and I continued playing. After this happened, for about six months, I followed all the rules.

Eventually, there were rumors in the school that I was a good dancer. People started treating me better. My teacher often asked me to teach other students in her class how to dance. Like my last principal, the Mamere began to treat me with more respect because of my dancing skills. The Mamere was proud to have me dance at special events in her school.

She had never had a student like me who excelled at something she enjoyed doing. It brought the school a lot of buzz and public notoriety. Word spread to other schools about my unusual talent. The administrator from another school came to the Mamere and asked, "Will you allow your daughter, Amira, to dance at our school for our event?" Girls of the school were considered "daughters" to the Mamere.

"Well," the Mamere pretended to contemplate the idea, "I'll think about it."

After two days, she said to me, "I would like you to go to another school and dance at their special event. Are you willing to dance in the public school for me? And you can take two girls with you, a teacher and two girls." She wanted me to represent the private school and present myself to the community. By doing these extra activities for the Mamere, I felt special and important.

I didn't excel in all of my classes. The only classes that I did do well in were the ones that had teachers that I liked. I got straight A's with them. They trusted me, respected me, and spoke nicely to me. When teachers didn't want me or were rude to me, I was awful. I had one teacher, Madame Tajee who, for some reason, didn't like me, and always made me sit in the back of the room. She may have been a little prejudiced because I was one of the very few that was not Catholic. Still, I did well in the class, except for tests. When we had a test, Madame Tajee would always give me at least a grade lower than my actual scores deserved. If my score warranted a B, she would give me a C-. This treatment continued throughout the class despite my protests. Each time I complained to Madam Tajee, she told me to sit back down. She always said, "I gave you the grade that I think you deserve. You will accept the grade, regardless of what you think you deserve, period."

It made me very upset, and I went to the Mamere and told her, "You know, I'm doing well. I don't know why I'm not getting good grades." I was failing Madame Tajee's class. Straight up flunking!

"Amira", the Mamere said, "If you're doing well, why are your test scores at a failing level? Your grades show that you're not doing well. Look at this."

"No. I'm doing well. I don't know why she gives me bad grades when I am sure that I'm doing well."

"Okay," the Mamere sighed. "We'll make a deal. We'll see what you do in the next two to three months. If you do well with your homework, I know it's not your fault. It's somebody else's fault."

For the next few months, I worked hard on my homework and was determined to show the Mamere that I was right. Our school did not let students do their homework at home. We had to do homework in front of them, so we did our homework at school during the evening. Under this close watch, I did well and received A's and B's. Yet, when it was time for a test, I did horribly. I felt intimated by Madam Tajee, and I began to realize she hated me for some reason. She would stand over me and stare down at me during the test. I couldn't even think of the answers I knew very well. On one test, I should have received a B, but due to her condescending stare and apparent disdain for me, I got a D-! It was easy to tell that she couldn't stand me.

I don't think she ever suspected that I was going to tell the Mamere on her. Nobody did that. Nobody! It always stayed between you and the teacher. Plus, the teacher was like a God at that time. You couldn't complain about the teacher to the Mamere and expect to come out victorious! The Mamere found out I did well on homework but never said anything to Madame Tajee about the test grades because telling on a teacher was not allowed. At least the Mamere now believed me and didn't kick me out of school. I didn't say anything about talking to the Mamere about the unfair treatment I received from Madame Tajee, but for the entire year, I complained to my family about her. "I don't like that teacher," I often grumbled. I told them Madame Tajee always called me stupid and dumb and unable to learn anything.

After I had enough, I didn't care if I got suspended from school or punished. When Madame Tajee called me stupid the next time, I glared back at her and told her, "You are stupid!" We continued this exchange with many insults back and forth. Whatever she told me, I gave it right back to her.

"I can't believe what you're saying! I can't believe what you're saying!" she said furiously. "Come here, come here! Come here!"

"No," I replied. "You come here, come here, come here."

She grabbed my hand angrily. "You don't talk to the teacher like this!"

"Take your hand off of me!" I screamed. I was so outraged too. I demanded, "Don't hold me like that!"

I pushed her hand away, and all the kids were saying, "You don't talk to the teacher like that. You don't push her hand away. You have to give her respect." I believe my relationship between Madam Tajee and me may have contributed to my anxiety and fear that she would be grading my tests. It seemed a reasonable explanation as to why I would always do poorly on her tests.

I don't think Madame Tajee told the Mamere what I did. I got away with a lot in private school. I loved my favorite teacher, Madame Seham, very much. She was a wonderful, kind lady. When people talk nicely to me and praise me, I feel like a real person, not an animal. She made me feel like I was worth something. Madame Seham always gave me praise when I did well. Whenever I did my homework in front of her, she said, "Oh my God, Amira. You're an amazing girl. You're so smart! I cannot think as you think." She always praised me for getting straight A+'s. I became very good at Arabic writing and felt very self-assured of myself in her class.

One day, we had a guest teacher in our school who was the dean of all private schools in Lebanon. He came from Paris, France, and his name was Mon Frere. If Mon Frere liked a particular school, he would teach as a guest. It was always an honor to have him teach at your school. His visit was something to be proud of because he didn't just go to any school. He was a critical man. When Mon Frere came to teach a French class at our school, I didn't know he was the Mon Frere that everyone respected. I had no idea.

As he was giving a French lesson to my class, I began whispering to my girlfriend. Mon Frere frowned when he noticed my nonstop talking.

"You," he said, "You, you! Keep your mouth shut while I'm talking," Mon Frere said sharply.

"Me?" I asked.

"Yes, you keep your mouth shut."

"No!" I said back. "You keep your mouth shut!"

Oh my God. Mon Frere's face turned as red as a tomato as he thundered, "Excuse me? Excuse me?" He was shocked. Nobody was supposed to talk to him like this!

Everybody in the class knew who he was. I had no clue, and I didn't care. I had no structural or emotional filter.

The kids next to me said, "Amira! Do you know who he is? Do you know who the teacher is?"

"I don't care! I don't care!" I shouted.

"Get out of my class," Mon Frere said in a calm, commanding voice.

"No," I said, "You get out."

"What?" he replied with disbelief.

Mon Frere insisted, "You get out now." Then he said, "You know what? I will get out right now!"

With that, he spun on his heels and stormed out of the classroom and went directly to the Mamere. He spent 20 minutes in her office. Meanwhile, all the kids in my class were afraid of what was going to happen to us. My classmates were all giving me advice before Mon Frere returned.

They asked why I acted the way I did. They pleaded, "Amira, please make it simple. What's wrong with you? Just take it easy."

"No! No!" I yelled and refused to listen to them.

When Mon Frere came back to the class, everyone was so quiet that you could hear breathing in the room. He stared straight at me, and I stared back.

"No, don't worry about it," he said, "It's okay. You can stay in my class."

He ignored me for the rest of the lesson like I wasn't in the class. It didn't matter to me. I didn't care. I had said what I wanted to tell him.

This is how I responded when I received authoritarian demands and strict rules. It didn't matter that it was the Mamere or the dean of the district. If I was asked to do something politely, I would do it willingly. Often the Mamere would tell me, "Your sister, Suead, is an angel, and you are a trouble maker. I don't know how your sister can be so pleasant and so different from you. Why don't you be more like your sister, Suead?"

The Mamere found it hard to believe we were related. She was right about how I was different than my sisters. Suead and Nada were perfectly behaved girls, and I was stubborn and demanded respect. Everyone loved my sisters. They were smart, did well in school, and respected everybody. I, on the other hand, couldn't care less what people thought about my behavior. I spoke up when I felt I needed to, and laughed out loud when I found something funny. I didn't like being told what to do. If you showed respect to me, I showed respect back. Being disrespected is why I usually fought. If anyone fought me, I would fight back fiercely.

At the end of the year, we had an important test to determine if we would move up to the next grade or repeat the class. I was confident I had done well, so I didn't worry. When the results came in, the principal and the teacher sat at the head of a table and passed out each student's grades.

The teacher commented to each student before me, "You made it. You passed. You received an A+. A+. A+."

Some kids made it through. Some kids did not. When it was my turn, Madame Tajee looked at me and said, "You repeat your class for next year."

"Me?" I asked, shocked. "Why?"

"That's the grade you got," she said. "You didn't do well. You failed the class."

I answered, without any emotion, "Okay." I think I was too shocked and stunned to say anything.

I didn't say anything to her even though the anger was quickly bubbling up in me. After all of the grades were handed out, I walked straight to the Mamere's office. Books in hand, I walked up to her secretary, sitting at the front desk. Everyone needed permission before being allowed to see the Mamere. Because it was the end of the school year, many students filled her office. The students were saying goodbye to each other. "See you! Have a good summer!" They hugged the Mamere. They kissed her hand and bent down and kissed her cross.

"I want to talk to the Mamere," I said to the secretary.

I demanded more loudly again, "I want to talk to the principal."

"You want to talk to the Mamere?" the secretary asked, with disdain. I replied that I wanted to tell her about the low grade I received from Madame Tajee.

Everyone who heard my loud voice wondered what was going on. It was very unusual for a student to complain about a teacher. It was not good for me, but that was the kind of person I was. I fought for what I thought was right. I wasn't afraid of anyone in school. The only person I feared was my Dad.

As I entered the Mamere's office, I spotted my teacher in the room. I immediately demanded, "Madame Tajee, come here." She walked to where I was standing. I also called out for the Mamere.

"Yes," the Mamere said as she looked back at me.

"Come here. I want to talk to you too."

"Yes?" she said and joined Madam Tajee and me.

When the three of us were all standing together, Madame Tajee looked at me like I was nuts. No one had ever done this to her before.

"I want both of you to know that I did very well in all of my grades. Look at my homework! I got A's and B's and A's and B's in all of my classes, but I did not get a passing grade for Madame Tajee's class. Can you tell me why I did not do well enough to pass? And why I failed? Why do I have to repeat the class next year?"

The Mamere snapped, "You're not smart enough!" She wanted to side with Madame Tajee. They always stuck together, no matter what.

"You're not smart enough!" Her taunt echoed in my ear. "To be smart, like your sisters, you have to study hard. You come from a good family."

Since she was the Mamere, everybody cowered in her presence when she spoke. That's how it was. I felt like they were ganging up on me and not hearing my questions. I wasn't getting any respect from either of them, but criticized instead for no reason. I turned to the only power I had. I still had my books in my hand, so instead of kissing her hand as others did, I hit her hand hard with my books. I pushed her and pushed Madame Tajee.

"None of you guys are fair!" I screamed. "And I'll see you someday!" Everybody was so scared! "What's going on? Oh my God! Amira!" Other teachers who witnessed the outburst were shocked about what was happening to the Mamere and the teacher. The Mamere went to her office and locked the door behind her. She was scared. I was only 13 years old, but I had a temper.

When we came home from school, Suead was crying and crying. She was so embarrassed. The woman standing next to Mamere outside of her office was the vice principal, and she had witnessed the entire confrontation. She told Suead, "I suspended your sister from the whole city of Byblos. No school will take her anywhere in Lebanon."

When my sister told me, I almost laughed. "Oh, this is a joke! You'll see me back at school!"

"Amira," Suead sobbed. "You're done with the family. You're a dead person."

At home, Mom saw my sister crying and asked, "What's the matter? What's going on? What are you crying for?"

"You have no idea what Amira has done!" Suead said. She told Mom the whole story.

"Oh, my God! Oh, my God!" My mom sobbed, "Amira, what did you do?"

Now we all wondered what Dad was going to do to me. Was he going to kill me? I knew I was in big trouble, and my Dad would punish me severely. Education was the thing that he stressed the most to all of us, and he did not accept insubordination at school. When my oldest brother, Adnan, came home in the evening, Mom told Adnan everything. We were all shaking about what my Dad was going to do. How would he punish me for such an awful embarrassment to our family? We had two days before Dad came home from teaching in the mountain.

"What am I going to do now?" Mom asked Adnan. "You know her Dad is going to kill her." My brother thought carefully. Finally, he said, "Okay, let's go to the school. We will talk with Madame Mamere and see what's going on."

The next day, Adnan, Mom, and I went to my school together. The Mamere didn't want to bother with us. We were nothing to her anymore. She didn't want to see me. She had no hope for me. You weren't even supposed to look into her eyes, and I had hit her.

The vice-principal came to talk to my Mom." I know the story," she said. My Mom just started crying! She couldn't hold it in. I couldn't hear much of the conversation because the vice president told me to stay away while she talked to my Mom.

"Yes..." I heard the assistant principal say, "She is spoiled because we let her get away with everything. Now, because of what she did, she will be suspended. I want you to know that no school will accept your daughter anymore. Do something about her. However you want to do it, take care of her. Give her whatever she needs, but she is not welcome here anymore."

"Please," my Mom cried to the vice principal, "Give my daughter a chance to do better. She was angry about Madame Tajee and blamed the Mamere." "No, it's not the Mamere's fault," the vice principal replied. "There is no excuse for your daughter's behavior and no excuse for her becoming violent."

It was Adnan who came to my rescue. My brother was brilliant, and he knew how to talk to adults. He showed the vice principal the highest respect and spoke politely.

"Look, I want to show you her homework." My brother showed her everything. He explained all of the assignments I had done all year long. I got good grades. The vice principal stopped talking and began listening to my brother's case.

"My sister said you suspended her, but I don't understand what's going on here." He pointed to the grades again.

After some time, she finally agreed with Adnan and said, "Yes, I see your point. I am glad you came to help me understand by showing me the facts."

After Adnan finished talking to her, he asked her to forgive me for my actions and pleaded for her to reconsider my suspension. After reviewing the facts, she agreed with Adnan that Madame Tajee was wrong. She corrected my grades to what I earned, and they let me stay in the school, and I did not have to repeat the class.

I proved I had been right all along. I don't know what they did with Madame Tajee. The assistant principal talked to Madame Tajee about falsifying my grades but did not suspend her. But I was no longer in her class. I was happy to be moved to another classroom.

I realized later that Madame Tajee was prejudiced. Not many Muslim students were enrolled in Catholic schools. My sisters and I may have been the only Muslim students enrolled. My sisters were never in Madame Tajee's class to experience her prejudice behavior. When I felt right about something, I wasn't afraid to fight for it. Without my Mom's pleading and my brother Adnan's support, I believe I would not have finished school for sure.

Chapter 7
Mom at the Hospital

Dad always picked on Issam because of his physical resemblance to my mom's brother, Ali, who Dad didn't like. At 16 years old, Issam was a sweet brother with the heart of an angel. He was honest and organized. Even though Dad picked on him, he trusted him. Issam always did what he said he would do.

One day, Dad told him, "I want you to plant flowers in the garden tomorrow."

Issam said he would, but he got busy doing other things and didn't have time to finish what Dad asked him to do. When Dad came home that day after working in Byblos, he asked Issam, "Did you plant the flowers as I asked you?"

"No, I didn't finish," Issam replied.

"Why not?" Dad's face was already getting red.

"I got busy and didn't have time," Issam shrugged.

Dad exploded. "You are such a dummy! I have not seen someone as dumb and stupid as you! You don't even know how dumb you are! Do you hear what I said?"

My brother looked straight at him, and he just ground his teeth and demanded, "What do you want from me?"

Dad almost laughed. "What's wrong? You chew gum just like a donkey!"

It was now Issam's turn to explode. "You know, I've had enough of you! I've had enough of you!" He lost his brain and his temper. "I've had enough of you! I've had enough of you!" he kept shrieking as he stomped around the room. Unlike me, my brother Issam showed his power. He showed his fist to my father. Issam wanted to punch him, but he didn't. Dad just stared at him. "Are you crazy?" Of course, Issam didn't hit Dad. Instead, Issam put his fist through the door that was between the kitchen and the bedroom. He hit it so hard that his fist went through the glass in the door. He didn't even feel it. He was so furious.

"Oh, look what you did!" Dad screamed. It made him angrier. "Look what you did!"

Issam just walked away. Mom came into the room when she heard the glass shatter.

"You son of a gun!" she yelled at Dad. "You're chasing your kids right and left! Leave those kids alone! You are abusing them!" Dad yelled at her, "You are the dumbest woman I've ever seen in my life! Get out of my face, dummy. I was stupid to marry you! I am sorry I married you!"

He began to hit her right and left in the face. The rope cracked against her skin like an oiled whip. It was the same rope we used as a leash for the sheep. Now he was using it on my Mom. He hit her in the face and on the legs. Her calves turned red. "Ouch!" Mom screamed. "Look what you did to me! Look what you did to me! How dare you do this to me?! You don't understand! You don't have any values for life, for women, for anybody!" He hit her even more.

It didn't matter what punishment she would get, Mom always tried to protect us. Dad beat her when she said something against him, and he didn't care if we witnessed it.

Finally, my mom got away from him, and she cried, "I'm going to leave you!"

"Go to hell!" he shouted.

She just walked away from him.

My Mom worked very hard to take care of us. She helped Dad build our house by hand. She took care of us, the house, and Dad's mother who was living with us. She worked in the garden, washed and ironed clothes, cooked delicious meals, helped with the building in Byblos, and sold milk and vegetables from the garden at home. She had so many responsibilities.

One day, Mom came to my Dad and told him she felt sick. She asked him to take her to a doctor. The doctor was a practitioner in Byblos, about 40+ minutes away from our house. Dad told her no.

"Please..." Mom begged, "Take me. I'm feeling sick. I don't want to die."

"No, I'm not going to take you," Dad replied. In a stern voice, he repeated, "I'm not going to take you."

"How can I go to the doctor?" she asked.

"Find somebody else to take you," Dad shrugged.

We were in the mountains at the time, and there were no other houses near us that had a car. The only way I can explain what happened next is that there must have been an angel around my Mom. There was only one taxicab that drove all day long. It belonged to Najie, the same guy who I previously gave a note for my Dad.

Beep! Beep! Beep! My Mom suddenly heard the horn of the taxi. We could easily hear the horn because our house was very close to the road. Mom jumped to her feet, ran outside, and yelled at Najie to stop.

He brought the taxi to a halt, peered out at her, and asked, "What's going on?"

"Please take me to the doctor," Mom said breathlessly. "I'm very sick."

Najee looked confused, and he asked, "Where is your husband?"

"My husband is not here," Mom lied. She always protected my Dad, no matter what. If we talked negatively about him, she would get upset with us. "That's your only Dad," she would say. She always stood up for him. She kept whatever was in her heart to herself and dealt with it in her way.

"Okay," Najie said, "Hurry up." Mom climbed into the taxi, and he drove fast to the hospital.

Mom stayed there for a few days. She had a severe case of pneumonia. She had been baking bread in the oven, and the mixture of heat, gas, and cold air may have led to her pneumonia. After her treatment for pneumonia, she developed bronchitis. She returned home to recover from bronchitis.

We were surprised Dad didn't take her to the hospital. His car sat in the garage for those three days. While Mom was in the hospital, my sisters and I stayed in the house alone with Dad.

"Holy cow," I whispered to my sisters. "We are with a giant now. He can kill us. I don't trust him. He can kill us."

Mom wasn't there to protect us, so we had to be extra careful. Even the smallest thing could set him off. If I didn't walk correctly, he would say, "You walk the wrong way. Come here. I want to hit you." He wanted to hit us for everything that didn't please him. He would come up with very creative reasons to hit us.

During those three days, I made sure to stay in my room and study. Dad always insisted I study before anything else. With my head buried deep inside a textbook, I pretended like I was studying. I couldn't concentrate though. I couldn't see the words on the page. There was nothing to see but fear. My brain only felt fear. I would just imagine...Where will he hit me next? Will it be on my back? Will he hit on this side or that side? Many times he hit us with no warning. Boom! Clap! Smack! Just like that, no warning.

Before Mom came home from the hospital, her brother, Ali, and his son, Hassan, visited her. Ali was the one my father didn't like, and he was well aware my father didn't like him. Regardless, Ali asked Mom if Hassan could stay for a few days because the young boy loved to be in the mountains. It felt to him like a cozy place, filled with trees, clean air, and wildlife.

"Sure, brother. It is fine with me." Mom said.

When Ali left the hospital, he took Hassan to our house and told Dad that Mom said it was okay for Hassan to stay.

Dad said it was okay with him too. He didn't want to say no. Dad had other plans for Hassan.

Since Mom was still in the hospital, Dad needed help to water the plants in the garden. He asked me to help him, and I said sure. Hassan was only four years old, so I took him with me.

I walked to where Dad was standing, with Hassan's small fingers tangled in my own. Dad stopped what he was doing, looked at me, and then looked down at Hassan. He had a long, thick hose in his hand for watering the vegetables. Dad continued to give Hassan a strange look. He walked calmly to the pomegranate tree and broke off one of the branches. It was a long, dark brown stick. He came back to where we were standing.

Then he started hitting that little boy for no reason. He hit him from top to bottom, from his head to his feet. Hassan was screaming bloodcurdling screams. His screams sounded like he was dying. Dad kept striking him so hard. I felt horrible. I can't believe what I'm seeing. He's hitting him for no reason. He continued beating him with no mercy. I just watched it. I kept asking myself, why is he hitting him? He didn't do or say anything wrong!

There was no reason, no provocation. Hassan was like a little butterfly, an agile bird. He just flipped over and over on the ground and tried to avoid the stick. There were so many strikes. Dad just kept hitting. Hassan tried to dodge the blows and dance around, but he didn't know where to go. Dad hit him in so many different places on his body; he had no way to turn to get away from them.

It was tough for me to be there that day. I was so young and helpless. It affected me so much in my life to watch that little boy getting beaten so severely. I couldn't protect him because I would be next, and what good would that do?

My uncle Ali never found out about that incident. That's the thing about little kids. When bad things happen to them, they don't tell. I didn't tell Mom about what I witnessed. I didn't even say anything to my siblings. I kept the fear and anger to myself. I thought it was safer for me. I just knew that if my Dad found out I talked about it, I would be in heaven somewhere. I felt that my Dad might kill me if I told anyone. I was scared. I had witnessed my sisters getting the same treatment many times.

A few days later, my Mom was due to come home. A bus brought people from Byblos twice a day. When its horn blared, "Beep, beep, beep!" from around the corner, I scanned the window for a glimpse of her. She always wore a white scarf on her head, and she liked to sit by the window. Sadly, I couldn't see her face or the veil on her head as the bus drove past our house.

Oh my God, I thought, when the bus didn't stop. My mom is not coming home today. It was four o'clock in the evening, the last trip of the day. My heart dropped like a heavy brick. I felt like somebody had taken me 100 feet under the ground and left me there. All I could envision was another day in hell. The whole world around me became dark, and I couldn't see anything. I knew Dad was there, but I didn't want to see anything. Darkness and sadness are what my siblings and I felt. We were scared of what else Dad was going to do to us before Mom came home. He knew we would never tell our Mom about how he treated us. He knew we would never talk. All I could do now was pray, pray, pray that Mom would come the next day. I couldn't wait for her to return home so I could be happy and feel safe again.

In the morning, the bus came again, and Mom was sitting by the window, wearing her white scarf. Beep, beep, beep! The bus blared again.

I had never heard a more welcome sound. She walked down the steps with bright, red balloons in her hands. She always brought us balloons or candy to make us feel good when she came home from Byblos. When she brought balloons for us, we swarmed around her like bees, skipping with happiness because our mother was finally back.

"I'm all right! I'm okay! I'm better!" Mom laughed happily. If Dad had hit me during this moment of joy, I would not have noticed.

Chapter 8
I am Worth Something

Looking back at my childhood, my Dad found little to like in me. And how could I possibly like myself with all of the negativity thrown at me?

I became very depressed. I always walked slouched over. I felt like I couldn't do anything that pleased my Dad. I tried to keep my back straight and do all of the things he ordered me to do.

One day, when Mom and Dad were in the city, and Grandma was watching us, she asked me to follow her.

"What?" I asked as I walked toward her.

As we went into the next room, she asked me to close the door. I didn't know what to expect because my Grandma was often mean to me. This time her voice seemed pleasant. She said, "I want to teach you how to dance." Of course, I was happy to say yes. She gave me slow and careful instructions. She put one foot in front of the other in a quick, graceful motion, and I followed each step. Very quickly, I learned how to dance. It seemed to be a natural talent that I didn't know I had.

As I got older, I became a better dancer, dancing every time I heard music that I liked. In particular, there was an Arabic dance that I loved. The dancer balanced a pitcher of water on her head. It took a great deal of balance and rhythm. I wanted to dance like her because it made me feel good and maybe I would gain the same respect that this dancer enjoyed. I was sure I could do it, so I got a pitcher, filled it with water, and placed it on my head. I was able to balance the pitcher on my head while I danced!

Even my Dad allowed me to dance. It was something that made him very proud. He loved my dancing. Whenever we had company, Dad would say, "Come here, Amira, I want to see you dance!" I was a little girl, so I would wave my arms and legs around like a monkey and do funny things. Dad actually encouraged me to dance, and he asked me to sing too. I sang when we had guests, and the people loved it. They crowded around me and applauded, and I loved the attention. It felt so good, like I owned the world. Dancing brought me a great deal of respect and admiration from people in the village. It was nice to have Dad admire something I did. I always dreamed he would look at me proudly.

In our village, we had a Chamber of Commerce. Every year, the Chamber of Commerce hosted a big party and invited several thousand people. When I was nine years old, the Chamber of Commerce invited me to dance for their annual party. Somehow, word had gotten around about a young girl who could dance very well.

I went to the party with my family. When the time came for me to dance, I stood before the vast crowd, amazed at how many people wanted to see me dance.

They announced, "Amira is going to dance for us."

The live band started playing music that I liked. I put a small pitcher of water on my head and started dancing on the stage. There were some steps, and I began walking down the steps to dance closer to the crowd. The steps were steep, and as I was going down, the pitcher fell and shattered on the floor. It sounded like a mini-explosion. The water went everywhere, and people cried out, "Oh Nooo! Nooo!"

I did what nobody expected me to do in a situation like this. I kept dancing! I didn't cry or run off the stage. I kept dancing as if nothing terrible had happened. After a few minutes, people stopped talking about it and just watched me. I kept dancing and dancing like crazy. In a way, it made the dance even more exciting. People forgot I had something on my head! They gathered closer and watched. There were many famous people at that party, including celebrities and important government figures throughout Lebanon. By the end of my dance, everybody felt I did wonderfully. Their enthusiastic cheers made me feel unbelievably good. Even my Dad didn't mention my mistake. He was so proud of me.

"Yes, she's my daughter! She's my daughter! Yes, she's good, isn't she?" he bragged happily to everyone.

My self-esteem went through the roof! For the first time in my life, I thought, Oh, I am somebody important. When I finished, people wanted to hug me. A group of them even threw me in the air and caught me.

"Oh, look at you! You did an amazing job!" everyone cheered.

I felt so good! I've never experienced such a thrilling feeling in my life again. I felt like I was finally worth something. It made me feel good that people felt proud of me. After that night, whenever my Dad wanted to go to places, like his friends' houses, he asked me to go with him.

"Why do you want me to go with you, Dad?" I asked. I was honest. "I don't want to go with you." I never liked to go anywhere with my Dad because I was scared to be alone with him.

"Well, I want you to go," he told me.

"No," I repeated.

"Yes, I want to show you off," he said more firmly.

"Okay," I agreed.

He wanted me to go so he could say I was his daughter, the one who could dance. If someone said they saw me dance and that I could dance well, Dad would proudly tell them I was his daughter. I bounced like an eager puppy and danced everywhere they asked me to. People loved to see me dance because it was unusual for a girl my age to be so skilled. I felt terrific, and Dad felt good. He was proud of me, and it was nice to feel safe around him and feel good for something. I was happy.

Strange Encounter

When I was ten years old, I had a strange experience. I was standing outside the house with my Dad around noon, a beautiful, clear day, and everybody was happy for some reason. I don't remember what it was. Maybe it was a holiday. Anyway, Dad was talking to me, and as he was speaking, he noticed I was looking away from him.

"What are you looking at?" Dad asked.

I pointed towards the sky, excitement quickly building inside me. "Look, Dad! I see a red truck!"

Dad peered carefully up at the sky. "You see a truck?" He looked at me like I had lost it. He asked, "Where?" "Over there. Look! Look! I see a truck," I screamed, pointing wildly at the flying truck in the sky.

It wasn't a huge truck. From where we stood, it appeared to be about 20 feet long. You could see the shape of a truck though. Dad shielded his eyes and looked at the bright sky. "Yes!" he finally said, his voice matching my excitement. "Oh, what is this thing?"

He called to everyone inside the house. "Come outside quickly, everybody! There is a truck in the sky!"

We all stared at the red truck hovering over us. It was an extraordinary sight. We had never seen anything like it before. After a short time, the vehicle just disappeared. Poof, it vanished as if it had never been there. We didn't know what happened. In those days, we didn't understand the concept of a U.F.O. I don't think that word even existed in Lebanon at the time. Even our neighbors had seen it. "What did we see? What was it?" they said. "It is crazy!" We were all a little scared, but it was an exciting time. It was real. As I grew older, I realized we had seen a U.F.O. We talked about the truck for a long time. I still remember it like it was yesterday. I felt good that I was the one who discovered the truck that everyone was so excited about.

Chapter 9
Amira the Teacher

When I was 15 years old, my Dad opened a school on the first floor of our home in the mountains to tutor students needing help with their studies. He allowed me to teach in his school. I was the only teacher in Dad's school. He brought chairs and tables to put in the room, enough for up to 12 students. I helped my Dad find students to teach in our small, makeshift school. They consisted of friends, family members, and neighbors. The students' ages ranged from five to twelve years old.

As a teacher, I was very strict. When my students didn't complete their homework, I hit them on the hand and spanked them. Even if they cried, I had no mercy for them. These strict rules are something I had learned from my Dad. It was weird because when I played with them outside of our little school, I played like their friend, like a carefree, young girl. I showed them so much love and affection.

On the other hand, when I was teaching, I couldn't even smile at them. That's how serious I was. Even Dad asked me not to be so hard on them. He said I could not treat them that way.

"No!" I argued. "They have to learn. I am here to teach them, and they are here to learn." It was unbelievable that, of all the people in my life, I was having this conversation with my Dad.

I charged $5 per student for admission each time they came to class. If my students came to school without their homework, I sent them home. I refused to accept their money if they were not doing well or improving in my class. I would tell them, "I don't want to take your money. Go home and don't come back until you bring your homework with you. I don't want you to waste your family's money for nothing. Give it back to your mom or dad."

I was a harsh teacher at times. If a student's performance was subpar, I hit them and made them go on their knees with their hands against the wall for two minutes. If they were doing poorly in my class, I kicked them out. I told them, "I don't need your money. Stay home. Somebody else can take your place."

Even as I was saying it, I couldn't believe what was coming out of my mouth. I was 15 years old and hungry for money, but I was fair to them and their family.

I cared about their schooling more than money, and the funny part is I was starving for cash! Still, I wouldn't take it. When I told the students they could not come back to school, they and their parents became distraught.

If they wanted back in my class, they had to bring their parents and money the next time they came.

The parents would always plead with me, "My child will do better. Give us one more chance. I'll help with the homework."

If I agreed, I would allow the student back and begin to collect admission money again.

I was strict! Some of the people I taught live today in the United States and still love me very much because they learned so much from me. I was tough on them. They had to play by my rules, but they learned a great deal. They still talk about how good I was as a teacher.

While I was still in high school, I enrolled in a class at Care Trade Center (CTC) to learn how to type. CTC was a trade school where students prepared for careers. I enjoyed typing and did outstanding in my typing class. When I finished the typing class, the teacher asked if I would like to teach typing to adult education students. They hired me because I was a speedy typist, and they trusted me. I accepted the offer and started teaching typing in the next class. I also was asked to work in the treasury department, making sure everyone paid their tuition on time and collecting money for the treasurer. Students had three weeks to bring money for their courses. If they didn't bring money within three weeks, I sent them home.

I was just as strict in this school as I was in my Dad's school. I asked one student, after three weeks, "Where is your tuition money? It is due today."

"Ma'am," he said timidly, "I don't have the money today. My Dad said he would give it to me tomorrow."

"Okay, tomorrow will be okay. But if you don't bring the money, you will have to go back home." He nodded.

The next day came, and he didn't have the money. There were no more chances to pay. I dismissed him from class and sent him home.

The owner of the school wasn't aware of my strict policies because he wasn't there most of the time. He was mostly in Beirut, taking care of a different school. I had the full authority over the money. I don't think he would have been happy if I let students attend classes free. I was aware that teachers' pay came from the tuition that I collected.

At CTC, I continued to be as strict as I had been in my Dad's school. No jokes or stories. Bring yourself to learn, and don't bring excuses instead of money. I didn't listen to students' stories or explanations. My policy was, only enroll in school if you can bring the money on time. If you can't, don't come. That's the way I operated, period. Looking back, I taught precisely as my Dad would have, and I didn't know better until I learned on my own.

Chapter 10
My First Love

Half of my teenage life was ruined by not thinking clearly. When you are a teenager, hormones, thoughts of love, and desires can get into your head and blur your thinking. Mom had a sister named Alaweki, and she had a son, Sammy, who was quite a bit older than me. Sammy was a frequent guest in our house. When he came to visit, he brought oranges, nuts, and birds for me. Sammy liked to hunt and catch big birds much in the same way as my brother, Issam, enjoyed doing. He brought birds to me because he knew I loved to eat birds, and it would please me. My mom was happy to cook them for me. I can't recall what type they were, but they were huge. I was 12 years old, and I was getting a lot of attention from a nice boy. It wasn't long before I started thinking I might love him.

Every Saturday, Sammy came to our house from Baalbek. It took him about 45 minutes to make the trip. At that time, he was studying to become a nurse. He was at least 20 years old, and I was only twelve. Every weekend, he would come over and spend the night at our home. He stayed in the guest room.

He would always greet me with, "Look what I have for you!" as he showed me his gifts.

I would gleefully respond, "Yes! I noticed!"

After about six or seven months of seeing him regularly, I thought I loved him. I didn't know what to do with myself. He consumed my thoughts. When I went to school, I thought of Sammy. When I sat at home, I thought of Sammy. Mom was aware of my growing moodiness, but she didn't say anything. I think she felt like it was about her sister's son, and maybe it will work out in the future. She may have thought we would get married someday when I got older. Cousins can marry in Lebanon.

For several years, my brain was all about love. It was one of the reasons I didn't do well in school. I had no idea what Sammy thought about me when we talked. If he didn't have something in his hands, I was disappointed.

I would ask him, "Why don't you have birds with you today? I thought you liked to make me happy."

After several years, he began talking to me differently. Eventually, he said, "I want to give you a kiss."

I didn't say anything because I didn't even know what that meant. I asked my sister what a kiss was. When I found out, I yelled at him the next time he came over.

"You want to kiss me?" I was mad at him for that and didn't talk to him for a long time. Still, I missed him.

As time passed, we began to talk again. I loved him more every day because he brought more birds, oranges, and things to entertain me. I loved him for that. When Sammy became more interested in me, he left his girlfriend and stayed involved with me. But as time went on, he saw that I was not mature enough for him. I was not the right girl for him, so he went back to his ex-girlfriend.

When he went back to her, it broke my heart. I felt sick all the time! I started having constant headaches. Mom asked me what was bothering me.

My answer was always the same. "I have a headache. I have a headache." I didn't tell my mom why I had a headache... I was heartbroken and still in love.

When it became clear I was not getting any better, Mom took me to the doctor.

"What's going on with your daughter?" the doctor asked her.

"I don't know, she shrugged. "She is having constant headaches."

"Come here," the doctor ordered me.

When I stopped in front of him, he said, "Put this book on your head."

I placed the book on my head.

"Walk across the room," he commanded. "Walk back and forth a few times."

As I walked, the book stayed balanced on my head and did not wobble.

After watching me, the doctor turned to my mom and said, "Your daughter is fine! She walks straight."

He scratched his head before asking, "Could it be that your daughter is in love?"

"I don't know," Mom said.

"You're the mother! What do you mean you don't know? You have to know about your daughter's feelings!"

Mom thought about it. "I don't know. I know she has somebody she talks to, but I don't know if she's in love. She's still a young girl."

The doctor got upset with my Mom. He said, "Well, I don't think you know about your daughter. I think she is in love, so you have to do something!"

"Ok, but he's no longer around her."

"He's not interested in her anymore? That's why she has a headache!" He was a brilliant doctor.

It took me about a year to get over Sammy. I wished I hadn't fallen in love with him. Maybe if I hadn't, I would have paid more attention to myself, my education, and been a normal kid. It was not the right time for me to fall in love. I didn't even know what a kiss was, much less what love meant.

One of the things I was most upset about is that my Mom didn't interfere when she saw the change in Sammy's feelings for me.

"Why didn't you recognize what I was getting into? You could have told your nephew that you don't want him to be with me!"

I wished she had recognized I was getting too close to Sammy and realized I was in love. She thought I would be fine, but I had a human heart just like everybody else! Anyway, she didn't say anything and Dad didn't mind. They knew that nothing wrong was going to happen, so they didn't care. They trusted Sammy.

When Sammy didn't visit, I asked someone who was going to see him to tell him I missed him when he didn't come.

He sent a message back that said, "When you see the moon at night, say hello to me."

"Oh, okay," I replied.

"You say hello to me, and I'll say hello to you."

"Yes," I said. Our relationship never got any closer than this.

The memory has stuck in my head ever since. Whenever I see the moon now, I remember Sammy. "Look, it's Sammy," I quietly say to myself. "Hello, Sammy." Sammy died ten years ago due to a kidney problem. He was my first love, and it was so much more than just about birds.

Chapter 11
Driving

I began feeling a little better when I started driving a car. I was feeling a little stronger just because Dad trusted me. I wanted to stand straight and tall for that reason. He was beginning to trust me a lot more.

One of the best things Dad ever did for me was teach me how to drive. He had a Volkswagen Beetle, and he had already trained Suead and Issam. I don't think Dad trained Adnan. He had no time to practice driving because he was always studying.

One day, Dad told me, "Well, I want you to know, someday when you get a job, I want you to use my car if you know how to drive." So he began teaching me how to drive.

Of course, at first I didn't do well. Whatever he instructed me to do, I nodded my head and said, "Okay." But he would get angry at my mistakes and smack me while I was driving. Boom! After that, I didn't want to drive anymore.

When Dad told me to turn left, I turned right. I went the opposite way. "Turn right," he instructed me.

"Turn to the right?" I asked. Okay, I thought to myself, I'm going to do it correctly. Instead, I went left. All of a sudden, boom! On my back! On my neck! Dad smacked me.

Oh my God, I thought, how can I sit and drive? If I'm driving and he hits me from the back, where are we going to go? I couldn't think under the threat of his blows. So I didn't do well.

The roads going up the mountains in Lebanon are very narrow compared to the streets here in the U.S. There is just enough room for two cars to get by. The curves were especially bad. You had to blow your horn before you reached the curve to alert oncoming drivers you were coming that way or else someone would come around and crash into you. Beep! Beep! The horns blared at every bend in the winding road.

One time, I was driving in the mountain with my Dad on a straight section of the road. It wasn't easy for me to drive a stick shift, going uphill. I needed to make a curve soon because a blind curve around the mountain was coming up. It was a narrow, winding, dirt road with barely enough room for two cars to pass each other. Only one car at a time went around the tight curves. You were supposed to blow your horn to alert an oncoming driver who might be getting near the curve that you were already there. When entering a curve, you always listened for a horn blowing, warning you to give them the right-of-way.

Dad reminded me, "Blow your horn before you turn at the next curve."

But I forgot to blow the horn, and before I knew it, I saw a huge truck coming towards the car. Dad screamed, "Stop!!" I pushed on the brake as hard as I could, and just froze in fear. Just when I thought we were going to crash, the other driver stopped. Our cars were only 20 inches away. It was a miracle we didn't die on that curve. I was waiting for the blows to my head.

Dad just stared at me for a moment. I thought he was going to hit me. Instead, he said, "You are doing all right. You are doing okay." Dad was upset with me, but he didn't hit me. I think he was just happy to be alive after the close encounter.

It was not only my fault. The other driver came around the curve too fast and didn't blow his horn either as he approached the curve. Dad continued to train me every day, little by little, whenever he had time. I slowly became a better driver, and he finally thought I could take the driver's test in the city. The driver's test was only 15 minutes, and he thought I could do well for that amount of time. If it were for 30 minutes, maybe I wouldn't do well. Dad had to teach school that day, so he sent one of our neighbors with me.

The man administering my test told me, "Okay, I want you to go up this hill." Three or four people were standing outside watching how I was doing. I started going up the hill, but I was going backward!

"Wait a minute, wait a minute!" the man yelled, "I asked you to go forward, not backward!"

"Yes," I said, and I went backward again. Finally, the man asked, "Why are you here?"

"I don't know. My Dad says I'm doing well."

I was scared to death my Dad would punish me if I didn't pass. I knew my driving opportunities would be lost.

My neighbor said, "Don't worry, she's nervous. She's nervous, and not used to driving my car."

The person giving me the driving test talked to me nicely to help me relax, and I began to do better. By the end of the test, I passed. When I came home, Dad was so happy to hear the good news and he told me, "When you get a job, I will let you use the car."

Finally, I felt as though I could do something right. I could not only dance, but I could drive a car. The Volkswagen was a stick shift and required coordination and practice. Finally, I was worth something.

My sister, Nada, was studying to become a nurse, and she knew many people in Lebanon. She told me about a job opening I could apply for in Tripoli. Soon after, I got the job. I was 18 years old when I started working there. Dad bought a Mercedes for himself and let me use the Volkswagen as long as I obeyed his rules. Dad expected me to tell him exactly where I was going at all times and how long I would be there.

Before letting me drive to my new job, Dad insisted on taking me there first so I could learn the route. He said, "I want to show you how to get there, and what to look out for." During the drive, he gave me very detailed and precise instructions. He not only showed me the route, but he also pointed out the busy roads that might be dangerous. He told me to blow the horn ahead of the curve to alert an oncoming vehicle. He insisted that I not drive too fast. He advised that many people here don't pay attention. "They drive too fast, and they don't use turn signals." He gave me all the directions and information I needed. "You do exactly what I told you to do. If I give you the car, will you do that? Can I trust you?"

"Yes, Dad," I told him, "You can trust me."

After he believed I understood his rules, and promised to obey them, Dad told me I could use the car to get to work. Until then, I had been using a taxi.

He said to me, "I'm going to let you drive the car to go to Tripoli today. I trust you now."

Tripoli is about 30 miles from Byblos, about an hour's drive. For me, this was a big trip. "Okay, Dad."

"But you must do everything I taught you. Promise?"

"Yes, Dad, I promise."

When it was time to leave to work, I drove off in the Volkswagen, and Dad went to the mountain in his Mercedes to teach, or so I thought. On this day, he took the day off. I had no clue that he didn't work that day. Little did I know that Dad was behind me, trailing the Volkswagen with his Mercedes!

I was driving to work when I saw a man hitchhiking along the side of the road. I stopped.

"Where are you going?" I asked.

"I'm going to Tripoli," the man answered. "Get in," I said and opened the door.

A short while later I saw an older lady waiting for the bus. She looked tired, and she didn't look like she had much money. My heart softened, and I stopped the car.

"Where are you going?" I asked.

"I'm going to Tripoli," the old woman replied.

"Okay, I'm going to Tripoli. Get in," I opened the door for her. "Oh, thank you!" She was so grateful. "You're so sweet!"

After that, I saw more people along the road while I was driving. They all got inside the car. Passengers now filled the car. Meanwhile, Dad was behind me, watching the whole thing. I had no idea. When we reached Tripoli, I dropped everyone off in their respective places and went to work. On my way back home, the same thing happened. I saw people along the side of the road, stopped for them, and asked them where they were going.

"I'm going to Byblos," they told me.

"Great, I'm going to Byblos too. Get in."

"Oh! God bless you! God bless you! I wish there were more people like you!"

I didn't charge any of them. I felt sorry for people in need. When I finally made it home, I noticed Dad wasn't back. He came home 30 minutes after I did.

"Hi Dad," I said when I saw him walk through the door.

"Hi, you made it! I'm so proud of you."

"Yes, I am proud of myself too."

"Are you doing well?"

"I didn't have any problems," I replied.

"Well, tell me now what happened. Did you go to work today?" Dad asked.

"Yes."

"Tell me exactly what you did."

I told him everything that happened. I told him about the people I picked up on the way.

"But would you tell me why you took these people with you? Did you know them?"

"No, I didn't know them," I said.

"How do you know they are good people? They might kidnap you or kill you."

"No, Dad, they wouldn't kill me!"

"Maybe they wouldn't, but I'm telling you, don't do that again. It's not good for you. You never know. Some guy could like you, and he might take you somewhere."

"No one's going to take me. I'm sure no one will take me."

After I had finished telling him about the day, Dad looked at me. "Well, one thing you didn't tell me yet," he said.

"What do you mean?"

"You forgot one thing."

"No, I told you everything!" I protested.

"No, you are not finished. I want you to tell me more."

"I forget. I don't know, Dad. I swear. Everything I know I told you about."

Dad looked at me. "Well, I told you when you see a curve, you blow your horn. Did you do it?"

"Oh..." I started, "I don't think I did..."

"You didn't tell me that."

"Well, I forgot."

"Well, okay," Dad said, "I forgive you."

"How do you know what I did?" I asked.

"I was behind you," he said with a big smile on his face.

"You were behind me? Where? Did you follow me? You didn't go to school today?"

"No," he smiled, "I took a day off just for you."

Oh my God. I was so shocked, my brain became numb. I thought my Dad was kidding. I didn't believe him until Mom confirmed it.

"Yes, he did," she confirmed.

"Now you have my approval," Dad said. "Wherever you need to go, be careful, just drive safely."

One day, my Aunt Jamilie asked if I could take her downtown because it would be less money than the taxi. I was so happy, but I was not sure if I knew how to drive well in downtown traffic. On my way to pick her up, I passed by a car close enough to hit him, and the guy yelled, "What's wrong with you?" along with some bad words. I felt like, what's wrong with him? I thought I was driving well. I also came very close to other cars, and I scratched a vehicle, but I kept pushing forward to pick up my aunt.

While driving my aunt to the downtown, I hit another car. The guy was trying to get me to stop, but I didn't.

"What did you do? Why didn't you stop? Do you know how to drive?" My aunt asked.

I said, "Yes, he doesn't know how to drive!"

Somehow, we arrived downtown. A few people saw me driving crazy, not caring, and driving the car wildly. They were yelling things like, "You don't know how to drive! Get off the road!" I thought I was driving okay most of the time. Even though I had been driving for some time, when there was other traffic, like downtown, I didn't do so well. I thought it was acceptable to hit cars and street poles and such.

When I got home after driving my aunt downtown and hitting several cars on the way, Dad confronted me and said, "I heard you are not driving well. What happened to the car? Show me."

I took him to see the car. There was a dent on the back and the side. I told him they hit me; I didn't hit anyone. I lied a lot. I learned to lie because I knew he was going to hit me. Fear, it was all fear. If I lied, I was protected. I wouldn't get hit anymore.

One day, I had a big accident. I went to my girlfriend's and dropped my sister off. I was coming back by myself, driving 80 miles per hour. I was very depressed and crying. I was in love with another boy, and we weren't getting along. I slowed down to make a left and thought I had enough time to make the left, but when I made the turn, everything went dark, and I didn't know what was happening. Everything looked blurry and dark to me. All I knew was I was going to the hospital. I didn't even think about myself. I was scared that Dad was going to hit me.

When they took me home, my brother, Fouad, came and made me a sandwich. I ate it, but it looked dark. I could not see what I was eating.

"Sister, you're in trouble," Fouad told me. "You are in trouble."

"I don't know what to do," I told him.

"I will take care of you."

Fouad was usually a troublemaker with my Dad. Dad said he would be back in two days. Everyone was worried about me, and they covered the side of the car with a white sheet. I was starting to feel better, but fear still filled my heart. When Dad came home, he didn't check the car, but he came up to me. He had already heard there was an accident. He didn't ask if I was all right or anything. When the neighbors saw that he had arrived, they all came over and said to him, "Do not touch your daughter. Don't touch your daughter."

Dad didn't say much, because by the look on their faces, he knew they were serious. My neighbors had that look like he would be in trouble if he hurt me. They knew what was waiting for me.

"Come with me," Dad told me.

We went to the car, and he demanded, "Uncover the car."

"No, I don't want to."

"Uncover the car."

I uncovered the car, and he looked and said, "Holy smokes! Oh, my God!" The car was totaled.

"Please don't hit her!" Everyone was trying to protect me. I think they protected me from getting a severe beating.

Then Fouad jumped in and said, "Don't touch my sister! I'm telling you, don't touch her!"

"Okay, you fix the car," Dad told my brother.

"Okay, I'll fix the car."

My brother gave me $500 to get the car fixed. One of my sister's friends repaired the vehicle. Fouad paid to have the car fixed, not my Dad. In any case, I was glad I did not get a blood clot in my brain or some other permanent damage to my body. I don't know why Fouad stood between my Dad and me. In my heart, I believed that, once again, angels protected me.

In 1975, a civil war broke out in Lebanon. I was working in Tripoli at this time. Certain places in Tripoli were affected by the war, and certain days of the week were worse than others. On Wednesdays, it was hazardous to travel there. You were a dead person if you did. Mondays were okay. I didn't know which days were bad and which days were good. Dad didn't know either. He thought I would be all right driving there, but he wasn't aware of how bad the situation was.

Because I had the Volkswagen, I was the queen of the neighborhood. My neighbors asked, "Amira, when you go to Tripoli, can you get me oranges and bananas?" Fruits and vegetables were a lot cheaper in Tripoli. I made notes of everything they wanted and brought back the items as they requested.

One day in particular was horrible. Dad didn't listen to the news because he was at school in the mountain. He didn't hear about "Death Day." It was a Wednesday and there was a threat of war. Soldiers shot everyone who went into Tripoli on that day. It didn't matter who you were or where you lived. I didn't know about the day either. The Syrian army was guarding the roads two at a time, but I didn't know.

I was on my way to Tripoli with my younger sister, Nada, on "Death Day Wednesday." We spotted a military person, and he waved his hand and ordered me to stop. If a soldier orders you to stop, you better stop. You cannot keep driving. If you don't stop, they will shoot you right away. He asked me to stop, and I did.

The soldier was a big man with long hair and a well-grown beard. He looked like the type of man who could kill people without hesitating. When we looked at his face, all we could think was, "Please don't kill us." The soldier was holding a big gun across his chest, with his finger on the trigger. He looked at me, and I smiled.

"Where are you going?" he asked.

"I'm going to Tripoli," I told him.

"What are you going to do there?"

"It's none of your business," I told him.

"Excuse me. What did you say?"

"It's none of your business," I repeated.

He looked at me very calmly as he put his hand on the window edge, and with a deep rough voice, said, "Pardon me?" He then laughed at what I told him. He could see I was stupid and naive. His laugh was the kind of laughter that said "you don't know who you're dealing with."

"It's none of your business," I said for the third time.

He stared at me and finally said, "Okay, will you be coming back this way today?"

"Yes, I will come back the same way."

"Okay, go," he laughed. "I will let you go this time."

When he told me that, I continued on my journey. After maybe one mile, another military soldier stopped me. I recognized this soldier. He was our neighbor for about three years until he moved to Syria. We had a strong relationship with him when he lived next door to us. He worked for the Syrian military. My mom used to cook food and take it to his house because his family still lived in Syria. We loved him, and he loved us.

"Oh my God, Amira??" he said.

"Yes, it's me!"

"I am surprised you are still alive." He was almost in a state of shock.

"What's wrong?" I asked.

"This is the day that people get shot going to Tripoli!"

"So what?" I shrugged. "What does that mean?"

"Oh my God!" he was angry. "What are you doing here? Nobody travels on this road on Wednesday! No one! Not anyone!"

Even prominent political people came heavily protected by bodyguards, and I was the only one who came like it was no big deal.

"Don't go back today!" my neighbor said. "It's very dangerous! It's amazing you are still alive!! Did you see the guy who has a long beard?"

"Yes."

"What did he say to you?"

"He didn't say much. He asked me where I was going. I told him it was none of his business."

My old neighbor almost exploded. "How dare you talk to him like that? He kills people for no reason! It's no joke! He takes them out of their car and shoots them alongside the road in a ditch. He simply shoots people. It doesn't bother him at all to kill someone he doesn't like. He asks them to follow him off the road and shoots them right then without any questions. That's the way he is. He doesn't negotiate with them. He pulls them out of the car if they don't get out. They beg, 'Please, please, please, don't kill me.' Then he will tell them, 'I'm not going to hurt you. Follow me.' He then shoots them when they go into the ditch. That's how he is. You are lucky to be alive!"

"Don't go back today!" he warned me seriously. "Don't go back in the evening! Both of you will be dead for sure! You're out of your mind! Didn't your Dad tell you about the rules and the danger?"

It didn't matter what our military friend said, I knew we couldn't stay in Tripoli overnight. I disregarded his strong warning and returned anyway. What's new about me not following the rules? But I knew we might not make it back alive. When we reached the place where the bearded soldier had stopped us, it was around six o'clock in the evening. The bearded soldier was not at the checkpoint. We were relieved not to see him again. A different soldier was there to stop people coming from Tripoli. He was kind to us, and let us go. I believe an angel was in the car with us.

When Nada and I got home that evening, it was dark, and our family and neighbors were worried about how long it took us.

"You made it home safely!" They were thrilled to see us. I then told them what happened.

"Oh my God, we heard it was a forbidden day to travel to Tripoli. You made it! We don't know how you made it. Did anyone stop you on the way back too?"

"Yes, one guy stopped us, but there was a different soldier who was not as violent."

Everybody heard of the first soldier who stopped me. They had heard about a bearded soldier killing people on the road to Tripoli. That soldier was renowned for showing no mercy. He was a cold-blooded killer. All my neighbors were scared to death.

"You made it!" My neighbors were saying, "Yes, you had Jesus with you. God was with you. You had an angel with you." Everyone shared more stories they heard about the soldier with the beard.

When Dad came home, he said, "I heard about your ordeal."

Despite everything that happened, I brought fruits, vegetables, water and bread, and other things my neighbors had asked for. "God bless you," they said. Everyone was happy, but more than that, they were relieved nothing terrible had happened to Nada and me.

I will never forget that day. It took me a while to realize just how much danger I had experienced. I didn't even know how lucky I was not to have been killed.

There was an angel in the car with us that Wednesday that kept us safe and unharmed. There is no other answer as to how we survived the trip.

Chapter 12
Suead Leaves Lebanon

I had a very close relationship with my older sister, Suead. We did almost everything together. She took me everywhere she went, and I had fun with her, as she had many more friends than I did. It was now 1975, Suead was 22 years old, and I was 18 years old.

A man named Afif came back every year to visit his family in Lebanon. He was attending school in the United States (Wayne State University in Detroit, MI), and he was an American citizen. Afif was previously married, but now he was single again. He had two sons from his first marriage.

Whenever Afif visited Lebanon, he stayed in his family's big house across the street from us. Afif wanted to find a Lebanese woman to marry and take back to America. Afif would often see my sister from his home when she was outside and he watched her whenever he could. He was very attracted to her, but Suead paid no attention to him. She was too focused on her education, but Afif's eyes were on her.

One day, Afif asked my Dad if he could talk to Suead. My sister had no idea. She was interested in someone else. It's not like she had a boyfriend or anything, but she had a friend. All she cared about was school. She wanted to finish college. Dad agreed to let Afif talk to her. After a while, Afif asked Dad if he could marry my sister. In Lebanon, parents arranged marriages. Dad agreed, because Afif was educated and said he would take Suead to America after they got married. Afif was a teacher in America. A teacher wanting to marry my sister was a real big deal.

Dad told Afif he would be interested in talking to him about marriage. Dad then told Mom, and she said, "No, I don't agree." Dad said, "Yes, you will do what I tell you to do." Mom had to agree because it was Dad's decision. Then he talked to my sister. Suead was not interested, but Dad said, "You can't say that. You must marry him, and in time, you will learn to love him. He is a good guy from a good family. It's a big deal if you marry him."

He convinced Suead, and she said yes. In reality, Suead had no option. She was afraid Dad would give Mom a miserable life if she didn't agree to the marriage. She said yes just to keep peace in the house. In her heart, she didn't want him.

When I heard Afif was engaged to Suead, I hated him so much. I felt like he was taking her away from me, and I wanted to spend my life with her. I was so jealous of Afif; I felt like choking him. When he walked somewhere with my sister, I walked between them. When Afif tried to walk closer to Suead, I moved closer in between them to keep him away. My brothers were also protective of Suead. Issam couldn't stand Afif. The marriage was so sudden. I was emotionally, mentally, and physically shocked.

It took a few months to finish the papers required to enter the U.S. We drove them to the Beirut airport, about an hour's drive. Many people went with us to see her off and wish her well. There were five cars full of people, I rode with my Dad. My sister went with Afif, his mom and dad and her best girlfriend. Our car was in front of my sister's car. I was sitting in the back seat, so upset and depressed. My sister was leaving me. I thought I might never see her again. The world around me was dark. I couldn't see any light.

Then I heard my sister's voice talking to her girlfriend. She said, "Oh, trust me, my friend. I will call you, I will write to you, and we will stay friends. I will love you the same as I do today. Maybe someday you will go to America, and we will be friends there too."

I was listening and thinking, "Oh my God, what am I hearing? Oh my God! I can hear my sister's voice in the car behind us!"

I didn't tell my Dad, Mom, or anyone. I kept quiet and just listened to her voice from the car. Every time I heard her voice, I got more upset that she was leaving. At the airport, everyone kissed Suead on the cheek and said goodbye. When she came to me, I didn't show her how sad I was that she was leaving. I gave her a kiss on the cheek and said goodbye. It dawned on me that it was real. I didn't tell her I heard her talking to her friend while I was in Dad's car. I just kept it to myself. Years later, when Suead came back to Lebanon, I shared what I heard, and asked if she told her girlfriend the things I heard, and she said yes. She was in disbelief. There was no rational way for me to hear a conversation in another car. I can't explain it either, but it happened.

On the way back from the airport, I thought, "I have another sister, Nada." I never paid much attention to her, though. My attention was always on Suead. After she left to the U.S., I got so irritated whenever I saw Nada. I was cranky with her when she talked to me. I'd hit and push her away. I didn't want her in my life. Every time Nada tried to come near me, I pushed her away. "Don't come any closer! I want my other sister!," I snarled at Nada. I rejected her because the sister I loved the most and spent so much time with was gone. I was very depressed at first, and then I became outraged. For six months, my relationship with Nada was not good.

I later cried and asked myself, "Why am I doing this to her?" I knew it was wrong to treat Nada this way. She was kind to me, but I did it anyway. With time, I realized Nada was my sister too. She didn't do anything to me and didn't deserve this treatment from me. Eventually, as I began healing from the loss of Suead, my relationship with Nada improved.

After Suead went to the U.S., I went to a psychic to see if she knew how my sister Suead was doing. I went with my friends and asked her to also tell me about my life.

The psychic told me, "You're going to be a special lady when you grow up."

"What does that mean?"

"You have a gift. You are a healer. You will heal people in the future. The spirits around you love you. You are talented and gifted. They like to be around you." My friends and I laughed at her words. We thought she must be a sick person. I didn't trust what she said, but deep inside, I knew I had something special. I felt it. She said my sister was doing okay, but she was not happy. I decided to see other psychics to see if they could see something else about me. To my surprise, they all said that I had unique gifts.

Suead had arguments with Afif because he was a lot older than her. He didn't treat her like she was 22 years old. He treated her like she was his age. He wanted to be the boss. She didn't have a good relationship with him at first. Also, Afif's ex-wife used to bring their two boys to visit Afif in their home. Sometimes, his ex-wife spent the night because she had two kids, and the kids wanted to spend more time with their dad. My sister got jealous and irritated. She kept things to herself and cried a lot. She had a challenging time, but she didn't tell us. From time to time, she mentioned it to her girlfriend in Lebanon, and her girlfriend told us. Mom heard about Suead not being happy, and she went crazy! She went to Afif's dad and cursed him and said to him that his son was not treating her daughter well, and they were not getting along. Mom cried and cried. Eventually, after a few years, Afif began treating Suead better, and their relationship improved.

Chapter 13
Struggles in America

In 1977, when I was 20 years old, the civil war was raging out of control in Lebanon. My younger sister, Nada, and my brother Fouad were both too young to live away from Mom and Dad, so they stayed in Lebanon. Issam was living and working in Abu Dhabi, and Adnan was attending college in Romania.

My Dad sent me to Abu Dhabi to stay with my cousin Samir, his wife, Hannan, and their two children, Lubna and Hadi, where it would be safer for me. Their house was huge. Hannan's sister, Taghrid, was also staying with them. Taghrid fled Lebanon when the war broke out. Taghrid was my best friend in Lebanon, and I was so happy we were together.

Samir was a residential building contractor, so I helped him with his business while I lived with them. I had the best time of my life while I was in Abu Dhabi. I was away from Dad and Mom, living with people who treated me with respect and loved me. I felt as free as a bird. I got lots of attention. I felt loved, and all the guys I met said I was pretty. Guys in Abu Dhabi wore long white robes.

One of the guys was a minister in Abu Dhabi, and he knew Samir and my Dad. He asked Samir if he could date me. My cousin told him, no, Amira doesn't date, and my parents would kill him if they found out he allowed their daughter to date. "Once she goes back to Lebanon, you can ask her father, but she is only visiting here." Samir didn't allow me to date because he had responsibilities, and Dad trusted him. If I went out with someone, and my Dad found out, Samir would be in trouble.

I was in Abu Dhabi for about six months when my brother-in-law, Afif, asked if I wanted to visit them in the United States. I really didn't want to go back to the abuse I endured at home, and I missed Suead, so I said yes.

The night before I was scheduled to leave for the U.S., Samir arranged for a big send-off party at a hotel. He invited Choukair family and friends from work, about 50 guests. There was dancing, live music and the best food. While I was dancing, I noticed a guy staring at me. I began to feel uncomfortable with his stares as he watched every move I made. He was talking to his friends and it appeared they were talking about me. I worried maybe they were planning to kidnap me when I left.

On my way to the exit, I saw one guy on one side of the doorway, and another guy on the other side. I knew if I ran away from them, they could surely catch me, so I began to scream.

"What's the matter?" someone asked.

I cried, "Someone is going to kidnap me!" Others asked, "What are you talking about?"

"Yes, I'm afraid those guys are going to take me away from here!

I'm looking at them right there! They are going to kidnap me!"

When the men saw me pointing at them, they suddenly darted off and ran away. Samir assigned two people to protect me. They put me in their car and had one car in front of us and another vehicle following us all the way home. We drove away really fast. It was around 1:00 a.m. and there were not many cars on the road. I was terrified all the way home. I later found out those men were horrible people and probably had been plotting to kidnap me. I believe it must have been an Angel that warned me to be afraid. I will never forget this scary send-off party.

When Dad heard about the incident the next morning, he said, "Thank God! Someone could have kidnapped you, and we would never see you again." He wished me well and hoped to see me soon.

The next day, my flight left to the United States as scheduled, and when I arrived safely, I was relieved. I felt like I was in a safe place. It felt like I arrived in heaven.

It was wonderful to see my sister, Suead, and her husband, Afif, and their first child, Zanobia, in Detroit, Michigan. Zanobia was five months old at the time.

Their house seemed like a nice place, peaceful and quiet. Some things I didn't like, but I didn't want to tell my sister or my brother-in-law for some reason. For instance, one day, when I was sunbathing in the backyard, a guy jumped over the fence into our yard where I was laying down. I thought he must be crazy, so I screamed as I ran into the house and locked the door. Fortunately, I was faster than he was and made it to the back door before he did. Suead heard me screaming and came running and asked what was wrong.

I said, "Nothing, nothing!" I didn't want to tell her. I was afraid they might send me back to Lebanon if I caused any trouble.

She pleaded, "Please! Tell me what's wrong! Something must be wrong!"

I decided against telling her that a guy had jumped over the fence and into her yard. Even though I was scared, I didn't tell her because I didn't want to go back to Lebanon. Eventually, years later, I finally told her.

After three months at my sister's house, Suead said, "You need to return to Lebanon."

I asked why, and she explained, "You are visiting here on a 90-day visa, and the visa will expire soon. Afif is going to Lebanon for a visit so you can accompany him."

I pleaded with her to let me stay two more months, but Afif said that would not be possible, and I must leave with him. I asked why, and he said, "It is better than you traveling alone."

No matter how much I pleaded with Afif, he insisted that I return to Lebanon with him. I had no choice but to go. My heart was in the United States, and I knew someday it would become my home.

When I returned to Lebanon, I told Dad I liked living in the United States. He asked me what was on my mind, and I explained how much I wanted to go back. Dad told me I was dreaming. He explained what he meant when he said I was dreaming. "You have to go to school here, and if and when you return to the United States, you will have to pay for your plane ticket."

In my heart, I knew I would be going back. Yes, the United States was a dream, but it was a good dream, and I knew someday this dream would come true.

Afif returned to the United States after spending about three months in Lebanon. With the help of Suead and Afif, I applied for my green card. It took about two years to be approved. Finally, my dream came true, and I immigrated to the United States in 1980.

During the two-year process, I didn't get along with Dad at all. I was teaching English at CDC. It was good for me because my English was improving at the same time. I earned money from the CDC and saved as much as I could.

Afif was a big help in many ways. He was so helpful in getting us to the United States. He sponsored me when I came to the U.S. from Abu Dhabi. Issam paid for the plane ticket, but Afif sponsored me and paid a $500 deposit to the American embassy. When we went to Lebanon, Afif got the $500 back from the embassy. That is how sponsoring works. He welcomed me in his home, and sponsored me and Issam to immigrate to the United States.

When I came back to the United States in 1980, I lived with Suead, Afif, and their daughters, Zanobia, Summer, Sarah, in Livonia, Michigan.

But Afif didn't encourage me to go to school, and he seldom praised me. He treated me like my father did. Afif would say, "You're not smart. You have a long way to go in life. You need more education."

Did I leave my Dad to find the same thing here in the United States? I could not take it anymore! When he told me I was not smart, I said, "You're not smart either." When he put me down, I put him down. When he told me I was not polite, I said, "You are not polite either." Everything he said, I said back to him. He quickly made me feel miserable and uncomfortable because he was unable to say anything nice to me.

To help with my living expenses, I got a job at a Big Boy Restaurant as a hostess. I thought I was doing a good job seating people at their tables. All I had to say was, "How many please?" and "Follow me please." I didn't always seat them where they wanted, but no one complained. I was very innocent and said yes to everyone I met at work. When men gave me their phone numbers, I always took it and said, "Thank you, sir."

The manager liked me, but he felt I was getting too much attention, so he sent me home and told me not to come back. I didn't know what I did wrong. I told Afif I didn't have a job anymore.

He went back to the restaurant where I worked and talked with the manager.

"I like your sister-in-law very much. I'm fond of her," the manager told Afif. "But she is getting too much attention from my customers, and she is not handling it well. It is becoming a distraction, so I don't want her here anymore." Afif told the manager I would stop taking phone numbers if he hired me back. He tried to help me, but it didn't work.

The manager was attracted to me and wanted a relationship. I think he got jealous because people kept giving me their numbers, and I kept taking them. I wasn't hiding anything. I always showed them to my sister. I was naive. I never called any of the numbers because I didn't know why they gave them to me.

I appreciated everything Afif did to help me come to the U.S., however, as the atmosphere in Afif's house became more cynical, I knew I had to move away. It reminded me too much of my life in Lebanon.

My brother, Adnan, was living with my brother, Issam, and Issam's wife, Mary, in Farmington. Issam offered to let me stay with them, so I accepted the offer. Issam worked at Montgomery Ward as a repairman in the tire shop. Then he got a job at a Coney Island Restaurant as a cook. He was not even an experienced cook, but he worked hard to learn as much as he could about the business. Mary helped him learn to cook the meals that were on the menu.

Because his English was not very good, and mine wasn't much better, we had a hard time understanding road signs and directions. We couldn't read or understand maps. Mary helped us learn how to survive. We had to crawl in this new world before we could walk.

One day, Adnan wanted to show Mary how much he was learning, so he went grocery shopping without her. He bought some canned food with a picture on the label that looked like a delicious beef stew, but it didn't taste as good as it looked on the can's label. When Mary came home later that day, Adnan presented the canned food to her for her approval. She first gasped and then began laughing. It caused all of us to laugh. When she collected her composure, she explained he had unknowingly purchased and eaten dog food!

Issam went into business with a partner for a Coney Island Restaurant in Wixom. He rented a three-bedroom apartment in

Wixom, very close to the Coney Island. I moved from Farmington to Wixom to live with him. Our cousin, Monzer, arrived from Lebanon and moved in with us. There were now five people in the apartment.

When I moved to Wixom, I got a job at another Big Boy Restaurant on 12 Mile Rd in Novi, Michigan. I worked in the kitchen and cut vegetables for salads. I had to go in and out of the walk-in refrigerator and freezer all day. Eventually, I got very sick. I couldn't handle the hot-cold-hot-cold. I could not work while I was ill, so I had to leave my job at Big Boy again. I was now out of work again! I didn't take care of my health very well. I ate junk food and smoked cigarettes. I used to smoke in Lebanon as well, but Dad did not know it. I was now smoking around 15 cigarettes daily. No doubt my unhealthy eating and smoking habits contributed to my health issues.

Issam had a lot going on in his life. He was tough with me, but I understood his attitude toward me wasn't all his fault. He got a lot of this from our Dad. He was struggling to make a living as a cook. He was getting around $5 per hour for a few years, then $10 per hour. I was not easy to get along with. I was stubborn and immature, and he could not take it anymore. He tried his best. Now he had to think about himself.

One day I walked from our apartment to his Coney Island and asked him if I could work there. It wasn't very far, so I didn't need a ride.

He said, "No, I don't want you to work here, sister, please go home." I felt rejected by Issam. I asked him why he didn't want me to work there. Issam explained, "When you come from a different country, you are different. You talk differently, and you laugh differently. It brings too much attention." He wanted me to simply visit and then return home.

I knew I had to improve my language skills if I wanted to get another job, so I enrolled in an Adult Education English class at Walled Lake Central High School. Adnan helped me a lot. He drove me to the class and picked me up when I finished. He was going to school at the time and never asked for money, but whenever he drove me anywhere, I always gave him gas money.

Issam didn't have much money, and it was difficult for him to save money because he had a lot of expenses providing a home for Adnan, Monzer and me. He also had the cost of being a married man. Issam was making a living, but he didn't have any extra money to save. He worked very hard. I appreciated him. I respected him for putting us in his house, and I was especially surprised he let me stay there. I gave him money when I could, but it wasn't much.

Adnan graduated from Wayne State University and got a computer systems job in Saudi Arabia with a ten year contract. He left his red station wagon for me to drive. I was happy that I could drive by myself! The car gave me freedom to come and go when I wanted to. It lasted until it got cold outside. It was below freezing. I didn't know how to take care of a car. All I knew how to do was put gas in it and drive. I had no clue I needed to check the antifreeze in the winter. The motor froze, and it was beyond repair. I was devastated and became irritable and frustrated. My cousin, Monzer, gave the car to a scrap yard for $50. My self-esteem was at another low point in my life once again.

One day, Issam asked me to go outside his Coney Island Restaurant to talk to me in private. He often took a cigarette break outside the restaurant. I had no clue what it was about but thought it must be important, so I followed him outside. As he was lighting his cigarette, Issam asked me why I was wearing my hair curly. I replied, "Brother, this is how I like it. Did anyone tell you they don't like my hair?" He answered, "Yes, my wife told me." I couldn't believe my ears! I yelled, "That bitch! She told you she didn't like my hair? I hate her so much! She is always mean to me!"

As soon as I said it, I knew I was wrong. Issam yelled back, "How dare you talk about my wife like that!" He was angry with me, and smacked me on my face so hard, I spun twice. I was shocked and scared. It brought back terrible childhood memories. It was one of the reasons I wanted to leave my father's rule. My brother had never touched me in anger before. I learned the hard way this is what you get if you cross Issam. I had no place to turn, no place to go. I no longer had the red car Adnan had given me. I had a brother who hits me just like my Dad did when I lived at home in Lebanon. All I knew is I didn't want to live like this again. I told him I was leaving.

He asked where I was going, and I said I didn't know. I was just leaving. I turned around and walked out into the street. I didn't know where I was going, and I wasn't sure how I was going to get there. I kept walking. I didn't have a clue where I was going. If somebody found me, maybe they would help me or let me stay with them.

Issam thought, "Oh my God. I have to follow her."

He left the restaurant and started to follow me, driving slowly behind me as I wandered down the street. It began to rain, and I asked myself, "Now what do I do?" I didn't want to go back to Issam's home.

I went up to a house and stood on the porch. I didn't know who lived there. I just stood under the awning to get out of the cold rain. As I was standing there, I was surprised to see my brother following me. He stopped in front of the house.

"Get in the car!" he told me.

"No!" I yelled.

"Please get in the car!"

I didn't want to, but I felt I had no choice. I got into the car and Issam took me to his home. I stayed the night, but we didn't speak to each other. Maybe he brought me back because he was afraid of what might happen to him if something terrible happened to me after he let me go. Perhaps he felt guilty for hitting me. All I knew was that I had to live somewhere else.

The next evening, Monzer gave me a ride to school. I asked one of my girlfriends if she knew somebody who would let me stay in their home. I told her my brother and I were not getting along, and I didn't want to live there anymore. I told her I was willing to clean houses and cook to help with the rent. She said, "Let me ask my brother. I'll let you know."

The next day, my friend came back to school and said, "Guess what? My brother needs someone to clean his house, and you might be able to stay there!"

I told her I didn't have any money because I wasn't working at the time. "Well, let my brother work it out with you. I'll take you there and introduce you to him."

When she introduced me to her brother, he asked me, "Where are you from?" I replied, "I am from Lebanon, and I have been living in the U.S. with my brother in Wixom, but we are not getting along well. I don't have any money, but I can clean your house, and I can cook. Will you let me stay with your family?"

He said, "You can stay, but I have two rules you must follow. Rule number 1: You must always be truthful and honest about everything. Rule number 2: Don't open mail that comes to my house." I thought this would be easy for me because I was an honest person. I moved in the very next day. I believe the anger that had been building up in me helped me be brave enough to live anywhere but my brother's house. I was on my own without help from anyone. I had no money and no job, and I was desperate and hungry. Monzer called Issam and told him I wouldn't be home after school. I had found a place to live near Wixom Road and Grand River.

I called my Dad in Lebanon and asked him to send me $60. He said, "Shame on you! You want me to send you $60, and you can work? How can you ask your Dad something like that?" I was in school and needed the money. I needed help from my family, especially when I left my brother's house.

Dad did not know I was very sick at the time and was flirting with death. I told death, "Leave me alone!" What helped me to stay alive was my inner strength, my faith, and my doctors. I told the doctors who were taking care of me I did not want to die. I wanted to live, and if I continued to live, I wanted to help people.

My cousin, Monzer, was attending Wayne State University and couldn't drive me to school any longer. He learned about my struggle and started to help me like a brother, as a father. Monzer would find time to bring me a hamburger and visit with me when he could. One day, I asked Monzer if he would call my brother, Issam, and ask him if he would loan me $50. He said to Monzer, "Tell her I would give it to a stranger, but not her. Tell her to go to hell. I'm not feeling sorry for her at all."

When I heard this, the anger inside me deepened. The only food I could afford was junk food. Monzer picked me up every Friday to take me out for dinner. This dinner became the only good food I would have all week. I would have eaten more healthful food if I had the money. Normally, I would never eat pork because eating pork is forbidden in my religion. Now, I ate anything available, any type of food to keep my stomach from hurting and provide calories. I was in survival mode.

I was struggling to stay in school and get good grades. Fouad told me I would never graduate from college, with all of the crawling I had to do, and the hurdles I had to climb. "You are working like a donkey for nothing. Why don't you go back to Lebanon and live with Mom and Dad? You can find a job there." My self-esteem was in the basement, but my determination grew stronger. I was determined to show everyone I was a survivor, and nothing was going to stand in my way. My life wasn't easy, but I was determined to go on.

I moved in with the family immediately. My room was on the third floor. It was a big, very old house with drafty windows and little heat. The living conditions were not perfect, but it was a place to stay where I was welcomed and could call home. Each morning, I got up and made breakfast for the three children and myself. After they went to school, I cleaned up the kitchen and put everything away. After breakfast, I fed the dog and cleaned up his mess. I then cut the grass if it needed it. I would then come back in and clean the whole house. At lunch, I made myself chicken soup. I struggled for a while. I kept crawling along my highway without a known destination.

After about two months, her brother came to me and said he didn't like my cooking or cleaning. He said, "I'm not happy with your cleaning, and you don't know how to cook the things I like. I want you to start paying rent." He asked if I could pay $25/month until I got a job. When I told his sister, she was sad for me. She came up with a plan for me to work for her. She said she would give me $5 per home, and when I earned $25, I would pay him. The next day, she asked her brother if he could wait for me to earn some money, and when I made $25, I would pay him. She didn't tell him I would be working for her. He agreed.

I began working for her the next day. She knew I also needed money for my personal expenses. I was cleaning 3-4 homes a day, so I had the money to pay him fairly soon. She told me to save my money for a while before I paid him, and don't let him know when I had enough to pay him. I agreed to do that.

One day, I was counting my savings on the couch when I heard the garage door opener making its familiar groan. It wasn't time for him to come home, so I didn't worry. When I saw him come through the door from the garage, I was shocked and froze. He went straight to the couch where I had been counting my money and sat down. He appeared to be reading something in his hand as he sat down. I was terrified he would notice the money. As he shifted his weight, the coins jingled next to him. I thought "I'll be looking for a new place to live in the morning." His words kept ringing in my ears, "You must always be truthful and honest." Over and over my mind was focusing on, "What do I need to pack? Will he let me stay tonight, or put me on the street this minute?"

Somehow, he didn't notice the money lying next to him in plain view. He went to his room, changed his clothes, and took the dog outside for a walk. As soon as the door shut behind him, I rushed to the couch and scooped up the money. I was so scared and my heart was pounding so hard. I thought it would jump out of my chest. My hands were shaking like a leaf. I scurried up to my room. I had saved about $70.

One day, everyone was out of the house except me. I went to the kitchen to prepare lunch. I started to make chicken soup when I heard the basement door open, and out of the corner of my eye, I saw the basement door swinging open. It was easy to know when the door was opening because it had a familiar squeak as it opened. I then heard footsteps that sounded like someone coming into the kitchen. For a moment, I thought one of the kids came home from school early and went to the basement. I was trying to rationalize what I had just witnessed. I didn't know anything about ghosts or spirits.

"You are back from school already?" I asked.

I thought I heard a quiet voice say, "No, she's not here right now." Then, I heard another squeak, and the door closed by itself.

"What's going on here?" I asked myself. I tried to ignore what I saw and heard. I thought maybe I was losing it. I finished eating my soup and started up the stairs to my room on the third floor. I heard someone walking behind me, as if someone was following me.

I turned around, looked straight down the stairs behind me, and asked, "Why are you following me?"

There were no people inside the house except me. I was terrified and afraid I would be hurt if I stayed in the house any longer. I went outside and stood near the porch by myself. While outside, I saw a big snake, about three feet long. I had always been terrified of snakes. I don't know how I got the strength and courage, but I grabbed the snake from the back of its head and threw it on the cement driveway. It died instantly. A second snake came out from under the old porch, even longer than the first. I grabbed it behind the neck and smacked it on the cement. The snake just lay there, it too was dead. I felt I had to deal with this situation as I dealt with others, that is, do whatever it takes to survive. I didn't have anyone to help me. The anger that had built up inside me after the treatment from my Dad, my brother, Issam, and my dire current situation, was taken out on the snakes.

One day, I saw a newspaper on the kitchen table, and in the classified section, I saw an ad that read "Rooms for Rent." There was an empty room on the third floor, and my landlord rented it to a lady named Jennifer, a waitress at Twelve Oaks Mall. Now I had someone to listen to me. I enjoyed having Jennifer around. I didn't want to tell the landlord about the strange happenings in the house. He might have kicked me out, and I would have no place to go.

When I came in from doing my usual outside chores on this day, I heard a girl screaming and sobbing. I called out, "Jennifer, is that you?"

I followed the screams to her room and found her inside the closet, crying. I asked, "What are you doing in the closet, and why are you crying?" She said she heard noises and voices when no one else was in the house.

I asked her, "What do you think it is?" She told me she heard some footsteps walking behind her. I said, "You too?" She was surprised I heard it too. I told her how I thought it was my imagination. She said she also heard steps in the kitchen, and the door had opened and closed by itself. She was glad I had told her. I finally dared to tell someone who would believe me. I told her I didn't tell anyone because I was afraid I would be kicked out. Jennifer told me she was leaving and began packing her things. "Maybe you can stay one more night, and you can find a different place in the morning?" I suggested.

The next morning, we talked to the landlord, and Jennifer told him about hearing strange noises for the past week. When I told him I also had heard them, he knew they were real.

Jennifer asked, "Is there something going on in this house that we should know about?"

"Like what?" the landlord asked. "I hear noises in the house. I heard someone walking behind me, but nobody was there. It could very well be a ghost," he eventually said. "It likely is a ghost."

When I heard what he said, I was shocked. I didn't know what a ghost was, but I knew it wasn't normal. Jennifer explained to me what a spirit was. Oh my God! What am I going to do now? Where am I going to go now?

Later that day, I became sick from eating too many beef jerkies that I bought from a party store nearby. The man at the store said he wasn't going to sell me any more jerkies because they were not good for me.

"You come every day to buy junk food, and it will make you sick. Don't you get an upset stomach from eating so much junk?" When I told him yes, he said, "Then stop eating them! Eat something healthy!"

My stomach hurt so bad that when I got back home, I called my sister and asked her to take me to the emergency room. I had severe stomach pain, and I was vomiting. She took me to the closest hospital. I was admitted for examination to diagnose my condition.

The next day I was released. They told me I had bleeding ulcers and an inflamed colon. I probably had Colitis from eating bad food. My digestive system was a mess. I wanted to get better so I could move out of that house. Suead then took me to Garden City Hospital, where they accepted government insurance. The examination at the hospital was more thorough than at the E.R. I stayed several days, and the doctors discovered the damage to my colon was very severe.

The doctors told me I was lucky, and promised me they wouldn't let me die. Five or six doctors were working on my case. They asked me many questions: "Did you travel overseas recently? What did you eat? What country are you from? Are you eating every day? Tell me about your breakfast. What did you have for lunch?" They were shocked at my answers that consisted mostly of beef jerkies.

I overheard one of them comment, "I don't understand how she is still alive." Then they came to my bedside and said, "Your case is a difficult one. We are not sure how to help you."

I had lost a lot of blood and was feeling dizzy. I didn't have enough strength to walk or even get out of bed. I told them, "I don't know what is wrong with me, but I don't want to die. Please don't let me die."

I felt there was a good chance I might die in the hospital. My only hope was my Guardian Angel would come to help me live. I prayed I wouldn't die. I was too young to die now.

My cousin, Hatam, told me the doctors said I might not live longer than a week. He asked the staff to move my bed to face east because it is a cultural tradition. He didn't want to tell me the real reason. Gravely sick people expected to die are turned to face the east. He told my family in Lebanon what the doctors told him. No one could believe the sad news. They replied in disbelief, "Amira is so young and so nice. How did such a thing happen to her? She's not going to make it?"

But inside of me, I knew I had strength. I was determined to make it. I was not going to accept death as an option. I continued to pray and gather all of my power to survive this massive roadblock to my journey. This obstacle on my life's highway was in the hands of God and the medical staff. All I could do was pray.

My stay in the hospital lasted six weeks. I lost a lot of weight. I was not able to walk or do anything. I was too sick to eat, and often it felt like I was at the end of my highway. My struggle to survive had come to an end. I thought I was heading to God, but again something inside me kept me going. I didn't want to die, and something in my soul gave me the message that I was not going to die. Maybe it was my Guardian Angel. Maybe she heard my cries and prayers. I was going to keep going.

While I was sick and recovering, I would often dream that people wanted to hurt me. I was on a mountain, covered with beautiful green pasture and trees with green leaves. I looked down the beautiful valley and saw my cousin, Essman, who died from cancer. He looked angry and began to hurl big stones at me. His rocks traveled about a mile and barely missed me as I ducked to avoid getting hit. He kept yelling from the valley for me to come to his world. The grass was also green down in the valley, but I knew that he was dead, and I didn't want to go to him. They were all people I knew who had already died.

All of the people I dreamed about were angry and wanted me to come to their world. I protected myself by flying away from the ones who tried to harm me. I looked back and saw that an angry woman was flying close behind me. I kept flying until I saw two beautiful crystal-clear ponds close together. I landed between them. The woman landed beside me. I noticed the pond on the right had dead fish floating on the surface, and the one on the left had live fish swimming around. I reached in the water to grasp one of the live fish, and at that moment, the woman behind me yelled, "Don't choose that fish! The live fish is not for you! The dead fish are for you!" I said to her, in a loud voice, "No, I don't want dead fish." I jumped up and flew away again.

I flew until I saw a huge golden building with a large gold entrance door that was guarded by tall, military-like guards who were Angels. The building appeared to be 500 ft high and a mile wide. I flew to the entrance. The guards opened the door for me, and I flew in. The door closed behind me. I flew from one corner of the room to the other, looking at all of the pictures of prophets on the walls. It was a beautiful place, like miles long. It had a very high circular dome made of shiny gold. The gold dome sat atop gold walls with massive pillars that seemed to hold up the dome. There were golden flowers of all types around the ceiling and gold doves in the corners. The gold was so shiny that you could see your face. The giant doors I flew through looked like they were made of bright gold with decorative silver designs.

I felt like this huge place was where prophets lived. Every time someone chased me, I flew to this vast, gold palace. Angels always opened the door and said, "You are welcome here." They always closed the door behind me after I came in. The angels let me visit pictures of the prophets, Jesus, Mother Mary, and Prophet Mohammad. The Angels told me, "You are with the prophets in their place." Finally, I felt like I was safe in this beautiful place where none of the angry people could hurt me. The woman who was chasing me was no longer a threat. I knew she would not harm me. I felt peaceful and safe. Then I heard a voice say, "Let her go."

All of a sudden, I opened my eyes, and said, "Oh my God! I'm still here!" The dream seemed so real, and now I wasn't afraid anymore. I felt love and peace. I felt like I was with my best friends. It was the message that helped me to remember everything. I then knew I wasn't ready to die. I was going to make it. I wasn't going to die. The one doctor who liked me assured me I wasn't going to die. He was right, thanks to the angels in my life.

I finally was released from the hospital. But it wasn't long before my condition flared up again. During another stay in the hospital, I was given steroid injections in my stomach and medications to control the inflammation, which had developed into Crohn's disease. I gradually felt better after the injections.

The healing was slow. I kept thinking about the dreams I had about visiting the prophets. It never left me and gave me hope and inspiration to go on with my life. I finally knew, without any doubt, that I was worth something. If the prophets thought I was worthy of living, I felt like I had something to prove. Getting healthy was a turning point in my life.

I continued to have dreams that guided me. I remember another dream that seemed to tell me to choose a positive path and to recognize the choices that would not be good for me. In the dream, a voice wanted me to visit the right place to get fish. The Angel's voice guided me to a big pool, brimming with fish, and the voice said, "Pick a fish." I picked a fish and said, "I want this one." The voice told me it was not mine, so I asked why? "Because it is a dead fish. You don't want that fish." The fish was red, like a dead one. She instructed me to select another fish. I picked up another that was lively and wiggling. The Angel said, "This is the one you want. This one is yours." Then I woke up. This dream inspired me to continue on my life's journey every day.

Much of my life's struggles, crawling down my highway, revolved around my medical problems. I was finally released from the hospital and went back home (to the haunted house with ghosts as companions!), where I lived for another 18 months.

I was so absorbed with the obstacles in my pathway, I had very little time to concentrate on my future. Every day seemed like a struggle to survive until the next day. But after being visited by my angels, I wanted to regain control of my life. I said to myself, "I can do it." Something inside me was keeping me going. Something gave me the strength to go on. I felt as though the angels were telling me I had a reason to live, and they would help guide my destiny.

I continued to have unusual dreams three to four times a week for the next ten years. I had a dream about my paternal grandmother, the one who I didn't get along with very well. She had been dead for about ten years. I dreamed she came to me, descending from above while I was sleeping and looked straight into my eyes. Her face was sorrowful, and she was holding a white dress-shirt in both hands. She placed the shirt over my body each time before she left. She never spoke a word in my dreams, and I never spoke a word to her. I never felt scared or threatened by the dream, but I felt compassion and concern in her eyes. It felt like the kind of grandma that I needed while I was growing up.

The landlord's sister decided one day she didn't want to clean houses anymore. So, I was without a job again, but I had learned to clean houses thoroughly. This experience would come in handy later.

Eventually, I found another place to live. I moved numerous times during the following two years. Novi, Commerce, Walled Lake, West Bloomfield, Livonia, Farmington, and Wixom. I moved from Wixom to Novi to live with a lady and her two daughters. I stayed with them for about a year. I had a variety of jobs, including washing dishes, cleaning houses, landscaping, working as a live-in companion, working in a group home, several restaurants, and more. I worked for anyone who would hire me. I had to eat, and I needed a place to stay.

Fouad was getting help from the Department of Social Services to help him support his family. He saw I was crawling down my highway. He took me to their office and encouraged me to apply. I refused to accept help from this agency. I wanted to make it on my own. They told me I could get food stamps and rent money. Still, I refused help. I was determined to survive in this country. It was my highway that I was crawling on, and I was going to make it myself.

I found an advertisement in the newspaper for a job at a dentist's office in South Lyon. The applicant did not need prior experience. The dentist was willing to work with someone who had an interest in becoming a dental assistant. I was excited to have an opportunity to work in a dentist's office. Working for a dentist was a big deal for me. It was a little far, but I drove straight there. It was a small office in downtown South Lyon. There were five people in the office: Dr. Healy, Dr. Linda, Andrea and Kathy at the front desk, and Kelly, his dental assistant.

When the dentist interviewed me, he asked basic questions. "Do you have any experience?"

"No, but I'm willing to learn."

"Okay, how much would you like per hour? I asked how much he was offering.

"How about if I gave you $3.50 per hour?"

"No," I turned down the offer.

He asked me, "Why not? Isn't it enough money?"

"No, I feel like I don't deserve $3.50. I will accept $3.00 because I don't have any training. I don't feel right taking so much money."

He looked at me and said, "I like your honesty. You're hired!"

"Thank you! I am ready to learn. Tell me what I need to know." Dr. Healy went over various instruments and procedures. I could see that Kelly, the other dental assistant, was very good at her job and he seemed to like her. She had been with him for two years.

After a few days of training, he put me to work, assisting him as he treated his patients.

As he was working on a patient's teeth, he instructed me to hold or hand many things to him. He asked me to place the suction tube on the right side. I wasn't sure what he meant, so I placed it on the left side instead. He looked as if he was going to kill me or hit me. He didn't want to show his frustration to the patients, so he nudged my arm toward the right. I still didn't get it. The first time he looked at me, I was like, what the hell? I thought it was a joke at first. Many times, it wasn't my fault. He told me to hold the light on the tooth he was working on, and I held it right where he said.

When he moved to another tooth, I kept holding the beam where he directed me to hold it. He turned his head toward me with an ugly scowl on his face and bumped me again. He didn't say I was supposed to direct the light when he moved to another tooth. He then told me where to stand while he was working on the patient. I became confused again and stood on the opposite side.

Every time I did something wrong, he bumped me with his elbow and whispered directions so the patient couldn't hear him scolding me. I kept trying to follow his directions. He had a peculiar look on his face, and I was like, oh my God, what does that look mean?

Somehow, I finished with the first patient, but I couldn't hold it in any longer. I went to the front waiting room and cried. I couldn't believe how he treated me when I did something wrong. The way he prodded me with his elbow and gave me such an angry face, I felt as though he was talking to an animal. I felt like exploding inside. The receptionist came to me and asked, "What's the matter, honey? What's the matter?"

"Nothing, nothing," I explained.

"Please tell me!" she repeated.

"He shouted at me and told me I wasn't doing anything right!"

"He tells me I'm not good either," Andrea said. "Don't worry about it. No one likes him. He's so picky; he is a pain."

Somehow, God was watching after me. I prayed he wouldn't fire me because I needed the job. He kept me with him for about six months before he told me, "I am going to have you work for Dr. Linda." Dr. Linda was very kind to me. She never told me I was stupid and always respected me. She treated me like a human being, and I enjoyed working with her. I was relieved. I worked with her for over a year.

Eventually, I got another job assisting a dentist in Livonia. This job kept me working for another six months until I got laid off. I was now able to collect unemployment until I found another job.

I had finally saved enough money to buy a car. Mary Shoucair, a family friend, sold me her car for $200. I didn't have enough money to buy the car, so Mary accepted payments. I paid $50 whenever I could until I paid it off. Now I could look for another place to stay and for a better job.

I applied for a babysitting job to help me earn some money to survive on. I interviewed with a lady, Christine, who lived with her nine-year-old daughter, Allison, in a large apartment in West Bloomfield. Christine had an office supply business in her apartment and needed someone to babysit her daughter while she was working. I got the job and moved in with Christine, her daughter, and her mother in West Bloomfield. The apartment was large but cluttered with office supplies. She paid me $500 a month, and I did not have to pay for anything there. I finally had a place to eat, sleep, and work. I stayed in her apartment for about a year, until Christine closed her business. She could no longer afford to pay me, so I got a live-in job with an elderly lady on Union Lake Road in Commerce Twp.

It seemed like my crawling would never end. I knew I couldn't get off of the highway at this juncture. There was no option for me. If I wanted to survive, I needed to keep crawling. Deep inside me, I knew there must be a smoother road ahead.

Chapter 14
Omar Enters My Life

One day, in 1987, as I was looking through a newspaper, I saw an ad for a church cross country ski trip, and it only cost $5. It was the first time I took a break from studying.

On the day of the trip, it was very cold. Everyone lined up to enter the bus that was taking us to the ski site. I almost decided to cancel my trip, but I would lose the money I had paid, so I stayed in line.

As we were waiting to board the bus, there were about 20 people in front of me. I had my big coat on but no gloves. A man got in line behind me. I didn't pay any attention because I was too cold. I had my hands tucked under my arms to keep them warm.

The man behind me said, "Excuse me, your hands are going to get cold with no gloves." I told him I would be fine. He then said, "If you hold my place in line, I have an extra pair of gloves in my car, and I can bring them to you."

I tried to talk him out of it, but he persisted. "Your hands are going to get too cold. I will get them for you."

He went to his car, got the extra pair of gloves, and gave them to me. I was so thankful. We filed into the bus, and as fate would have it, his seat was next to me. The man asked if it was okay if he sat next to me before he sat down. He seemed like a nice person, so I said yes.

"Miss, you have a cute accent. Where are you from?" he asked.

"Lebanon," I told him.

"Really? My Dad is from Lebanon."

"Where about?" I asked.

"I don't know. I was born here, and I don't know much about Lebanon." He introduced himself as Omar, and I reciprocated the gesture with my name.

A short while later, we made it to the ski lodge. There was a help-yourself, heated counter in the center of the room and seating around the walls. "Can I get you something to eat?" I asked.

Omar said it was kind of me to offer, so I stood in line to get him a hot dog. I brought him a hot dog with mustard on it, as he requested. He appreciated it. After we finished eating, Omar asked if I needed to get my ski equipment. I told him I was going to walk instead of ski. So he went to get his ski equipment.

When he reached down to tie his ski boots, I volunteered to lace his ski-boots for him. He said he was grateful and appreciated my help.

I followed Omar down the ski trail, and, when he fell, I helped him get up many times.

"Can I see you sometime?" he asked me later.

"If you want,'" I said. "I study at Dunkin Donuts three times a week. You can see me there."

Omar began showing up at Dunkin Donuts when I was studying. He got a coffee, and we talked while I sat at the table studying next to him. I was determined to get through school, so I didn't focus on him very much. Eventually he asked if I wanted to get something to eat at a nearby restaurant. I agreed, and we went to a Middle Eastern restaurant. He knew I didn't eat meat, and I likely would find something Middle Eastern to order. I remember that we both ordered Greek salads on our first date. We also went for pizza or to Wendy's or Big Boy Restaurants on other occasions.

I liked to take long walks several days a week. It helped me gather my thoughts, and it was relaxing to be alone and meditate while walking. I didn't care how cold or hot it was, or if it was raining or snowing. All I knew is that it was something I liked to do.

The next time Omar asked me to go out somewhere, I told him that walking was my favorite thing to do. He asked if he could join me. I wasn't sure I wanted anyone accompanying me while walking. This was my private time, but I decided to agree, just once, to see if it felt okay. He didn't look like the athletic type who enjoyed long walks.

Well, if he didn't like walks, he didn't show it. I enjoyed his company the first time we walked together. It was fun to have him with me, so I invited him often. It was now the middle of winter and very cold. I decided to walk one day during a massive snowstorm, with deep snow on the ground. I was sure he wouldn't accept my offer to join me this time. To my surprise, he agreed! We walked for miles, in blinding snow, around the entire lake that he lived on, and on to the next town. He offered a shortcut across the lake to get back to his car, but I was enjoying our time walking together, and preferred the long way. I remember him trying to keep his glasses clear of snow and icicles that were forming on his mustache. I think that's when it dawned on me that, for him to endure this torture, just to spend time with me, he must like me.

Omar's mom lived in Dearborn, Michigan, in a cute, small house. I got a warm, cozy feeling as soon as I entered the front door. When Omar introduced me to his Mom, she fell in love with me. She wanted to hug me right away. I never gave or received a hug from anyone before. I wasn't familiar with hugging. Even my Mom and Dad or other family members never hugged me. I asked myself, "What is she trying to do to me?" She would say, "Honey, come give me a hug." I walked up to her, and she put her arms around me. I just stood in front of her with my arms hanging down to my side. I didn't know what I was supposed to do. I guess Omar's Mom was expecting me to hug her back. I said to her, "We don't hug in Lebanon. I don't know how to hug." My mom, occasionally, would kiss me on the cheek, but that's it.

The second time I met Omar's Mom, she hugged me again. It gave me a beautiful, warm, comfy feeling. I started liking it more and more as I got used to it. I felt safe with his Mom. She liked my innocence and honesty. She began saying, "I love you. Drive safely," when I was leaving her house. No one had ever said "I love you," before Omar's Mom. It made me feel better about myself. Someone felt like I was okay. I had low self-esteem, but Omar's Mom didn't know it. She thought I was strong, but in my heart, I was down. I didn't want to show my weakness. I kept all my secrets to myself.

I shared the experience of hugging with my sister, Suead. She didn't know what a hug was until I showed her. She thought it was a strange thing to do. She didn't understand the affection it conveyed. And, when I said, "I love you," she didn't know what I meant. Expressing love in public was new to me and my sister.

Marriage

Omar and I saw each other for over a year before he proposed to me. He proposed to me in a non-traditional way. It was different, but it was his way. He asked in a polite, straightforward way, "Would you like to get married?" I felt like I was ready to be married. We agreed it was the right thing to do. Omar was different from others I had met. Omar didn't kneel or beg. He wasn't sure if I expected him to propose properly, and I didn't know what proposing meant. It wasn't a tradition in my country to propose. Traditionally, they have arranged marriages. Omar and I talked a lot about our similarities and differences. He learned about me in America, but he didn't know much about the rest of my life. I didn't know much about his life either. I knew he had two sons. Tony was 15, and Omar Jr. was 18. We knew we liked each other and had fun together. Omar had an older sister, Linda, a younger sister, Lila, an older brother, Joe, and a younger brother, Jack. We had fun when we visited them at family gatherings. I enjoyed dancing at their parties, and everyone treated me like family.

My brother, Fouad, lived in Inkster, Michigan, which wasn't far from me, but we didn't get along very well. My sister, Nada, was still in Lebanon and my other brother, Issam, lived in Grand Rapids, Michigan. I was not getting along with Issam, either.

Omar confided he didn't have the confidence to believe that I would like him. He said I was too cute to like him, or too good to be true. He said I was like a diamond in the rough, and you don't find one every day. He said his challenge was to not let me get tarnished or broken, but allow me to develop and shine into a precious jewel.

I was 31 years old and Omar was 46. I never thought about our age difference. It was just that Omar was kind to me through thick and thin, sickness and health. He never left me when I became sick.

We were not thinking of having a big, expensive wedding. Neither of us cared about that. We had our marriage ceremony performed in late December 1988, by a Muslim Imam at a hall in Dearborn. We didn't have much money when we got married. His sister, Linda, gave him a diamond ring to give to me, and his brother, Jack, was the best man. His other sister, Lila, let me wear a beautiful wedding dress that her daughter, Rhonda, had worn at her wedding. Rhonda did my makeup. The Imam performed our marriage ceremony with about 25 family members and friends in attendance.

We spent a week in Florida for our honeymoon. When we returned, we moved into Omar's home.

I had never seen Omar's house until we got married. He had a beautiful wood-burning stove, and brand-new furnishings in his home. He was making monthly payments on the furniture because he financed $5,000 for the couch and matching chair and $1,200 for the ornate stove.

As soon as I walked in the front door, I said, "That stove has got to go. And the couch has to go too."

He said, "I bought this new furniture for us."

I said, "No. I want to choose the furniture for us." Omar wanted to make me happy, so he let me buy all new furniture.

He sold the furniture for a couple of hundred dollars and continued making payments on it. It was hard for him when I came in and said that the stove and all the furniture had to go. But Omar agreed because he was a very good guy, and he did not want to have little things get in the way. The good news was his house was in West Bloomfield, a nice area by the lake, with a lot adjacent to the water. His house looked nice inside, but I changed everything in the house anyway. I hated the neutral colors. He agreed with most things that I demanded to be changed.

Omar's son, Tony, lived at home for a few years before he moving into his own apartment. His older son, Omar Jr., lived in his own house and had his own business. I didn't expect my two stepsons to like me as a stepmother. They were nice and very quiet. But I felt they did not like me as their stepmother because I took attention from their father. I also needed attention for myself. They seemed jealous of me.

Sometimes, I got irritated because they did things around the house that I did not like. I did not agree with all the things they wanted to do, so they weren't happy with me. I got upset, and Omar got upset. There was an obstacle between my stepsons and me. I didn't know better. I didn't have enough experience. They expected me to be a mom, but I did not know how to be a mom. I was more focused on my own life. If I knew more about children, I would have been a better mother for them. Sometimes we had arguments about his son, Omar. It almost caused us not to have a good life together. Eventually, my relationship with my stepsons got better as we began to understand each other. Life, as a close family, felt good.

I never had kids because of my Crohn's disease. We tried to have a child, but shortly after my pregnancy was confirmed, the fetus miscarried. I still think about how my life would have changed had my child survived. Sometimes I cry when I think about it. On the other hand, I was a very sick person, and may not have survived the ordeal of childbirth. I didn't think I was going to live very long as it was. Positive thinking and fighting my disease were the best ways for me to go on. I didn't want to die. I had to use all of my strength to keep going. There was still so much for me to do. Sometimes, I wished I had one daughter who was mine. Maybe I will have a granddaughter from one of my stepsons one day.

Omar bought me a beautiful, black Lincoln Town Car. This car became my favorite car of all time. I still think, today, about how special and proud I felt driving this big car. Omar always liked Lincolns because they were big and safe. He said, "If a big car crashes into a small car, the big car wins." We lived in a big house, and life was good. I spent a little of what I earned and saved the rest. Omar had the best car, though. He bought a brand-new Ford conversion van, which cost approximately $40,000. Omar liked to spend money on the things he loved. Even if it was for me, he wanted the best he could buy. He said, "While I'm here on this earth, I want to enjoy life while I am alive, and able to do so."

I continued to work and attend college after Omar and I were married. Omar made good money, but I wanted to work to make sure we could continue to live well. I found a catering job at a Middle Eastern restaurant on Northwestern Hwy. I served large groups of people at weddings and parties from 6:00 pm to 3:00 am.

I also applied for a companion job for an elderly lady. Her daughter interviewed me and asked if I was willing to clean and cook for her mom. I said, "Yes." She said, "Let me talk to my mom because you seem like a nice person, and I think my mom will like you." This job taught me a lot about caring for older people. I didn't realize that I was good with older people until I started working with them.

I also was hired as a companion at the Jewish Community Center (JCC) apartments. I loved the people I cared for so much. There was much for me to learn about Jewish traditions. When I was asked about my accent and what country I was from, I was afraid they might not hire me if I told them I was from Lebanon. So when someone told me my accent sounded French, I acknowledged I was French. Another asked if I was from Italy. I answered, "Yes, you are right. I am Italian." They were white lies that I thought were necessary to keep my job.

When I washed the dishes, the ones used for meat were washed separately from ones used for fish dinners. The same applied to taking them out of the dishwasher. Meat dishes went on a different shelf than fish dishes. The people I cared for were older residents with various needs, habits, and issues that developed with growing older. Some had diminished memory. Others had special needs like medications at certain times, being aware of foods they couldn't eat, TV shows they didn't want to miss, etc. I found out I could cope with all of the needs, regardless of how difficult the person was.

I cleaned, cooked, and took care of all of their needs at the JCC apartments. I wasn't very good at cooking the food they liked, but I did my best. They were quick to tell me the food was too salty or had no taste. Aside from cooking, everyone loved me very much. They loved the way I cared for them. I treated everyone with respect. More caregivers asked me to help them take care of their loved ones. They heard about me from other people. Word of mouth was getting around.

Another lady asked if I could work with her mom. She heard I was a good companion for elderly people. She asked, "Can I introduce you to my mom to see if she likes you and doesn't have a problem with your accent?" I agreed and we went to meet her mom. She and I got along very well. She said to her daughter, "She is so cute, and I love her accent." Her daughter hired me on the spot.

Although I was good at the necessary things, it was the little things that were most special to the caregivers. I was friendly and truly enjoyed talking to their loved ones. I always listened to their stories and encouraged them to express their feelings. I was genuinely interested in learning about their younger days and what they liked most as they were growing up.

As I learned about their likes and dislikes, I was better able to keep their interest in activities. What was most interesting was hearing about the kind of work they did. Many times, they would recall in detail all aspects of their careers. They would go on and on about their various jobs. The work I did with elderly people paved the road ahead for me. It was a rocky road at best. I still had much to learn, but I found out what I was good at.

I began to realize what I had a passion for, and where my career was headed. I began reading about Alzheimer's Disease and became interested in caring for people with dementia.

As my career began to develop, my relationship with Omar started to wane. Omar was a brilliant engineer, a genius, but he spent the money he made. I had no control over him. If I questioned him about what he bought, he got frustrated with me. He thought I shouldn't ask him about his spending habits. He was fair. If I could have changed his spending habits, I would have. Omar was still generous with me, but sometimes we didn't think the same.

Because I was born in Lebanon, what I believed in, I believed in strongly. I didn't have an open mind. My view was black and white. Omar was American and had a different way of thinking than I did. He was much more flexible and tolerant, so we had disagreements. There were some things we both did that the other didn't like. We didn't know what to do with each other, and it was not all one person's fault. It was both of us. I think I could have done better, but I didn't know better. I was still maturing. I was in college, brainwashed from my Dad's treatment in Lebanon.

It seemed like we were not compatible with some things. Also, I felt different living with a man. Marriage was new to me and I didn't know what I was supposed to do in this country. Anyway, Omar was an amazing man. He was very knowledgeable about life and American culture, but with me having only a little knowledge of his life, I did not know how to work on it. I just didn't want to be married anymore. After just over a year of marriage, I asked Omar for a divorce.

Divorce

Omar agreed to our divorce, which was final in February of 1990. Although we were divorced, he did not give up on me. He treated me well, respected me, and loved me as if we were still married. I got very sick, but he always loved and cared for me.

Even when I moved back with Christine in her West Bloomfield apartment, Omar stayed in close contact with me and looked after my needs. Unfortunately, my sickness put my love for him on the back burner. I still loved him, but with being so sick, I could not think of loving anyone. I was worried about dying. We were still friends for about five years, and he continued to bring me many things while we were friends. Occasionally I went to his house to visit.

My stomach was always in pain. I felt a little better after taking medication for my Colitis, but the pain got worse when I got stressed out. I would go back to the hospital whenever I became too stressed. I would stay for a couple of days due to excessive bleeding and pain. I tried to manage the stress, but I didn't know how to begin. It was like everything in my life was mixed up. It was all up to me to get better. I had to resolve this one on my own. The anger didn't come out easily. I was born a happy girl but I was abused as I was growing into womanhood. I had many stressors growing up in Lebanon that caused outrage and fears. I used to get excited when I thought about what life In America would be like, out from under my Dad's rules. But now, I was sensitive to anything that might cause stress in my life again. When I saw stress coming back into my life, I couldn't take it.

I remained determined and said to myself, "You know what? I will keep going. It's all up to me. As sick as I am, I must keep going." No matter how rough the highway became, I felt as though there was no option for me. If I wanted to reach my destination, I had to keep crawling. I tried to hide my sickness from everyone. I didn't want anyone to feel sorry for me. I wasn't looking for pity.

Eventually, Christine said she could no longer afford to have me live in her house without paying rent. I found an ad in the newspaper for a live-in housekeeper for an elderly lady in Union Lake, which wasn't very far from the college I was attending. I worked for her to pay for my room at her house. I washed clothes, cleaned her home, and cooked meals for her.

Omar and I had our differences, but we were also alike in many ways. We were both growing. He was still learning how to treat me better, and I was trying to learn to treat him better. When it comes to relationships, it takes two. Everything comes from two people, not just one. When people love one another, it takes two. When people get into a conflict, it takes two. Omar was awesome. He provided me with everything I needed to fulfill my dreams, and then everything started coming to me.

Meanwhile, my Mom and Dad were having problems in their relationship. My Mom was often sick and needed medical attention. Her heart condition caused her ambition and energy to diminish. She could no longer work as hard as she once did. My Dad began spending more time away from home. He started seeing a younger woman who lived in Baalbek. Our culture looked down on divorce but allowed a man to have more than one wife. On the other hand, a woman cannot remarry without consent to divorce from her spouse.

My Dad eventually married the younger woman and lived in the mountain home with his new wife. My Mom stayed with my younger sister, Nada, in the Byblos house. My Mom had many friends to help her through these dark times. They visited, brought her food, and comforted her. She hoped that someday she and my Dad could get back together. It never happened. My Dad and his new wife, Ensaf, conceived a child, Lubna. My Mom eventually came to the reality that she and my Dad would never reconcile their marriage.

Mom comes to America

In 1994, Mom decided to move on with her life and come to America. We were all excited to have her close to us again. We detested what my Dad had done to my Mom after she faithfully served him for 44 years. My sisters and I shared keeping her in our homes, but she mainly stayed with me. Issam began sending money to Mom so she could have her own money to spend. He continued to send her money every month until she died. My Mom and I lived in several homes until Omar helped us get our apartment in Farmington Hills.

My Mom loved the Chatham Hills apartment. She loved to walk through the expansive complex laced with flower gardens and manicured landscapes. Along the way, she made many new friends.

Everyone loved my Mom. When we were young, in Lebanon, Mama never forgot us when she went shopping. We looked forward to her return because among the food was always some form of a treat. It wasn't only candy, although candy would have been fine. Sometimes it was a balloon or other small item she could afford. She loved to see the exuberant smiles on her children's faces. We felt the love in her heart.

Now that Mom was living in America, the roles reversed. She loved the Kit-Kat advertising on television and often asked if I could buy her some. When I returned home with the candy and saw her broad smile, it immediately brought back an emotional childhood memory. I now know how she felt when she saw our smiles, and she knows how we felt when we received a treat. She always kept a stash of Kit-Kats to give to grandchildren when they visited, or anyone she met. My Mom loved to see smiles on their faces. Mom's love transcended the generations and oceans. We still feel her love today, and our love for her will never end.

Re-marriage

Omar continued to visit us in the Chatham Hills apartment often and took me to the hospital whenever I was too sick to drive myself. I kept working and crawling. My highway was strewn with sickness, a broken relationship, caring for my Mom and working.

After going through my sickness with me for over six years, I said to myself, "Oh my God, I like Omar better now. He stayed with me through thick and thin and sickness and health, good times and bad times. He is a good guy."

I think he liked me better too. We talked about getting back together for some time and eventually decided, after a six-year separation, to get remarried.

In August 1996, we were remarried. We had a quiet wedding. There were only 10 people at our wedding ceremony in Dearborn. We moved back into his house, the one I never liked. My mom moved in with us too. I thought she was going to stay for a few months and then move back to Lebanon. She would often say to me, "I want to go back to Lebanon, I want to go back to Lebanon," and I believed her.

My Dad and Mom talked on the phone very often. When she mentioned she wanted to return to Lebanon, things changed between them. Mom asked him to send her some money and he refused. He said, "Let your children take care of you. I don't have money to send you. I have a new wife and child to take care of. You are out of my life and out of my will." Mom decided she had no place in Lebanon anymore. Mom lived with us for seven years. She liked Omar very much because he treated me well and was kind to her.

Mom developed issues with her heart and failing kidneys as she aged, so I had to take her to and from the hospital regularly. During a colonoscopy procedure, the doctor perforated her colon. As a result, the routine colonoscopy became emergency surgery to save her life, and instead of being an outpatient visit, it became a 2 month hospital stay. We took care of my Mom through her good and bad times, and all the while, I continued with my education and career goals.

Chapter 15
My Education in America

Although my education and career changes cross-pollinated most phases of my life in America, I am dedicating a chapter that will span the variety of highways I had to traverse to realize my dreams. My dad wanted me to be a dental hygienist, but I wanted to get a degree in business. Parents can pressure you, brainwash you to do what they want. Dad did not want me to waste my life while in the United States. He encouraged me to finish my education. He wanted me to be a daughter that he could be proud of and brag to his friends. I applied for financial aid and was qualified. I had to do well in college and get all passing grades because if I failed a class, I'd be kicked out of the program and must pay for the failed course. I couldn't mess up because many other people were waiting to get in. So I studied hard and used tutors to help me.

Oakland Community College (OCC)

I attended OCC while moving from place to place. I don't know how I found time to study with all the chaos in my life. One thing I know is it wasn't easy.

I felt out of place at OCC. My accent was noticeable and sometimes students laughed when I said something in class. I didn't want to speak because I was afraid of being ridiculed. Students were rude and said I was simple and naive. No one wanted to be friends with me or even walk with me. I felt so alone and out-of-place, but I kept going. My self-esteem was at a low point, but my inner self told me to keep crawling. I didn't do well at OCC at first. I did okay in social science, but I didn't do well in nutrition. I remember the teacher, Mr. Zemke. I failed his class. I took the course again, but I failed again. The teacher didn't like me.

After I failed the second time, he told me he didn't want me in his class anymore. I asked him where I should go, and he said, "I want you to go somewhere else, but not in my class." I asked him if another teacher offered the same class on the same day, and he said, "No, you have to wait for another class to be offered." He asked me strange questions, such as where was I born, did I live with Arabs in Dearborn, and what religion I was, etc. He made me uncomfortable. I now know his questions were inappropriate, and maybe he was prejudiced. I think I failed because he did not like me. Now I was required to repay the government loan because I failed the class.

Deep inside of me, I didn't know if I was smart enough to finish my college degree. My brother, Fouad, said to me, "You have too many problems in America to go to college. Why don't you go back to Lebanon and help your mother around the house? Maybe Dad can help you with your education." My confidence was shattered. But I knew I had to keep crawling. I worked with several tutors to improve my comprehension. Each tutor gave up on me, left and right, because I needed a lot of work. Finally, I found a tutor who didn't give up on me. This tutor said, "It might be the language, the accent. Maybe that's why the teacher doesn't like you. You know what? I will send you to Mr. Gary, a nutrition teacher in the next room. Maybe he will be a better teacher for you."

I registered with Mr. Gary's class on Tuesdays and Thursdays. I knew this was my last chance to move on. The innate fear that was inside of me made concentrating on my studies difficult, but I liked this teacher, and he was patient with me. I finally crawled past my fear and passed the class with a B grade.

Wayne County Community College (WCCC)

I earned 60 credit hours from OCC before transferring to Wayne County Community College (WCCC). I heard WCCC had a better dental hygiene program. Every year, about 500 students applied for their dental hygienist program. If the judges chose you to attend dental school in the first year, you were lucky. If they didn't, you had to wait for an opening.

When I went in for my interview in front of the judges, I opened the door, and one of them said, "Oh my God, she's cute!" I was so relieved. Somebody said something positive about me! I felt relieved, secure, and safe. They asked me lots of questions, and I had so much energy that I answered them all with ease. I asked the judges what they thought about me, and they all said yes. I felt like I won the top prize at American Idol! They voted to accept me into that year's Dental Hygienist program. I felt like the luckiest person on earth. I was one of 100 students picked for the program. I was excited and danced all around, and they said again, "She's cute." From this point on, I was determined to study even harder.

There were 35 students in the class. I felt good because they respected me. I felt close to them. We were all going for the same goal. I told my friends to call me Amy because it was my nickname. It was easy to remember, and it was cute. With a name like Amy, I didn't

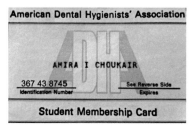

American Dental Hygienists' Association

AMIRA I CHOUKAIR

367 43 8745
Identification Number

See Reverse Side
Expires

Student Membership Card

feel like an outsider. I felt almost like an American. I was motivated to make it in America. I studied hard and hired a tutor to help me with chemistry. Tutoring and studying helped me do well in college.

My school friends were mostly African-Americans. They took me to the University of Michigan Library in Ann Arbor to study. They talked to me a lot, and, if they were short on change, I always helped them. I was around them so much that after a while, I felt like part of their family. I was very naive. In Lebanon, people around me were all Lebanese, a culture that I understood. Now, my friends were all referred to as African-Americans. I didn't know what that meant, but I could see they all had dark or olive-colored skin. I looked in a mirror and realized I have olive skin like some of my friends. I gazed for a while and contemplated maybe I was African-American too. I was bewildered. They talked about white people, like, "She's a white bitch." But they loved me. They took me to their favorite restaurants and brought me to their homes. I ate with them as if I was part of their family.

My dental hygiene classes at WCCC were not easy for me. I had to get a grade of C or better, or I would have to pay back

AMIRA CHOUKAIR

WCCC-DENTAL HYGIENE STUDENT

the financial aid I received. I knew I could not afford that, so it motivated me to do well. But I couldn't seem to keep up with others during class. As the teacher explained something, I was still trying to figure out the last thing she said. Once I got behind in understanding, the fear in me became intensified to the point that it was unbearable. My mind froze. Fear of failure caused me to focus on being punished instead of what I was trying to understand.

When I didn't understand something as a child, my Dad punished me for it. When I approached a classroom door in Lebanon, fear came over me. I was afraid to say anything to the teacher when I didn't understand the assignment. Fear of being hit and ridiculed in front of my friends caused me to freeze.

Now, in America, I carried this fear with me. I knew my Dad wasn't here to punish me, but the fear followed me. I began taking notes during class so I could try to figure out what was said when I studied after school. I knew I would have to focus every minute I possibly could on catching up before the next class. When I studied over and over, I could understand the work and remember it. I couldn't begin my homework until I figured out what the teacher said in class. I didn't always have time to get through everything. But, the things I learned, I learned well. When my friends studying alongside me needed help, it made me feel a hundred feet tall to be able to also help them.

The teacher gave us a test, and I didn't do well on it. Everyone got their test back, and if the grade was lower than a C, you were in trouble. She looked at me, then looked at the paper, and said, "Amira, come here please. I want to ask you some of the questions that are on this paper. Do you mind answering them?"

I felt like I trusted her and she wanted to help me, so I agreed. She asked me the questions, and I gave her the correct answers.

She said, "Why did you get the answers wrong on your test paper, yet when I ask you the same questions, you know the right answers? What's going on? Amira, something's wrong. Is something going on in your life? Would you tell me?"

I told her I had some fears because of my Dad. I explained how my Dad used to hit me when I didn't understand something. He would call me a dummy and punish me if I did poorly in school. She said, "Do you know if your Dad lived here, he would be in jail? Since you gave me all the correct answers when I asked you for them, I will give you a good grade." She reviewed my test and gave me an improved grade, and I was so grateful.

Later, she said to me, "It's going to be alright. Just keep studying, and you will do fine."

I was in school or studying my homework, with no breaks. I didn't participate in any school events. One day, a school friend asked if I wanted to join in a special event where the students could show off their cultural, artistic talents. I didn't know what it was about, but I told them, "I can do an Arabic dance." I was sure they would like my dance because I danced a lot when I was growing up. They asked me to show them what I could do. I showed them how I danced, and they went crazy. They loved it.

When I danced, I garnered lots of attention and became popular at WCCC. I was "the girl, the princess." People were walking by, some were playing music, others displayed cultural objects from their countries. There was a girl from India wearing an Indian costume and dancing a traditional dance from her country. I'm sure I did well because a big crowd gathered around me, and everyone was clapping with the music. Many people were taking pictures and videos as if I were a celebrity. I felt like I owned the world. Students noticed me more in school after that exciting event.

The next day, I had to come down from the clouds and get back to work, studying, and crawling. I transferred to another WCCC location, in Downtown Detroit, where they offered the courses I needed. WCCC offered courses in Detroit, Southfield, and Downriver, and I went to all of them.

One winter day, I was on my way to WCCC in Detroit. It took a long time for me to get to the campus, especially when the weather was terrible. My Guardian Angel was traveling with me this day. The campus was on Greenfield Rd in Detroit, and I was coming from Wixom. I was on 1-96, the Jeffries Freeway, near Newburgh road, during heavy, rush hour traffic. There was a lot of snow on the way, and it was very icy. Suddenly, I saw all the cars around me sliding. Cars were going left and right, sliding and spinning all around. I was terrified. "Oh my God, what is happening?!" I was afraid I would end up in a ditch, or be smashed by the out of control, spinning cars all around me.

I was so scared that I couldn't even scream. I couldn't steer my car and just left it up to my guardian Angel to guide me through a narrow, weaving path between wrecked and spinning cars. I made it through the traffic. My car came to a stop on the other side of the wrecked vehicles. I couldn't believe that I passed everybody. It was a miracle. I wasn't hurt at all, so I continued driving to class. A guardian Angel was the only thing that could have saved me from having a severe accident.

Help from My African-American Friends

Many friends who I studied with lived in poor, scary neighborhoods in Detroit, mainly made up of Hispanic and African descent. Omar wasn't happy to see me driving myself to study with my friends, so he offered to drive me there and pick me up after I finished studying. Omar drove me each time I went to study in Detroit. We would go to one friend's home on one day and another one's house the next day. He drove me to my study group on the deepest side of Detroit, Springwells Street. The area was multicultural with Hispanics, Blacks, and Puerto Ricans. There were lots of abandoned buildings, many with no windows. One of my classmates was living in her house with no windows. Anyone could get inside and take her stuff, and she lived with her daughter. I told her I didn't want to drive by myself and asked if it was okay if Omar dropped me off and picked me up.

We usually studied until around 10:00 at night. One time, before Omar began dropping me off, I got petrified. After we finished studying, I went out to put my books and homework in my car. Guys were riding around on bicycles with hoods over their heads. They slowed down and stared at me as they rode by. That was too scary for me. I told my school friend about it when I returned to her house. She wasn't afraid at all. She said they were friendly people. I cautioned her to be careful, but because she had lived in this neighborhood all her life, she felt safe.

My African-American brothers and sisters helped me traverse the rough terrain that was ahead of me as I crawled on my highway. They were my guiding light down the darkest roads of my journey through life. My highway was filled with many roadblocks, twists, and turns that I had to navigate, many unfamiliar paths. I didn't know enough to be afraid of the dangers of walking alone at night. I thought everyone was my friend and wouldn't hurt me. I was like a fawn walking up to lions, without fear.

The college that I attended on West Fort St was not in a safe location in Detroit. It was after 10:00 pm when my last class finished. Fortunately for me, there were guys in my class who knew the dangers lurking in the dark parking lot, and, for my safety, insisted on escorting me to my car. They were always polite to me and never expected anything in return. They treated me as part of their family, and I always thought of them as my brothers. I thanked them for protecting me. I didn't realize how much I needed their protection during my journey.

When I entered my chemistry class on the first day, I sat near the front of the room. Everyone else, except for one guy, was sitting at the rear of the room. I sat two seats from him in the front row. When I sat down, I saw a scar on his face from his ear to his chin. He didn't say anything to me in class, but in the cafeteria, he did speak to me. I was sitting by myself, studying for the next lesson when he walked up to me and asked, "Is anyone in our class bothering you?" I said, "No, why do you ask?" He said, "Well, if anyone does bother you, just let me know, and I will take care of it for you". I replied, "Thank you very much. What is that scar on your face from?" He replied, "Someone came from behind me while I was walking alone at night, and reached around me and cut my throat."

When he reached his hand up to his throat to demonstrate what happened to him, his shirt raised and exposed a shiny gun tucked in his belt. I had never seen anything like that before, so I asked him what it was. He said it was a gun and he used it for protection. Everyone in class avoided him because they knew he was a gang member and could be trouble. I wasn't afraid of him because I didn't know better.

He always treated me with respect. One day, he asked me if I would be his girlfriend. I told him, "I'm sorry, my father won't allow me to have a boyfriend." He asked, "Does your father live close by?" I told him Dad lived in Lebanon. He then said, "Just don't tell him we're dating." I said, "He will find out from my family. They will tell him as soon as they find out, and our culture will not allow me to date until I graduate from college." He accepted that and never mentioned dating again.

On the day of our final test, he came to me in the cafeteria and asked if I was ready for the final exam. I told him I was nervous, and I might not do well. He asked what grade would make me happy. I said, "Oh, I don't know. I think I would be happy with a C. He replied, "Don't worry. You will get a C." I asked, "How do you know that?" He said, "You told me what grade you wanted. Just take the test, and you will get a C."

When we got into class, he walked up to the professor and whispered something in his ear. I don't know what he said, but he was pointing toward me when he said it. He then lifted his shirt so that the chemistry professor could see his gun. The professor looked right at me, and nodded, as to suggest he understood what the student said. When we got our test results, I looked at my grade, and it was a C. I was so happy I didn't fail this critical class. If I failed chemistry, they would kick me out of the dental hygiene program. I was willing to accept any help to keep me crawling on my highway.

Since my lifestyle and eating habits had not changed much, I became deathly sick again. I was living in a Chatham Hills apartment in Farmington at the time. I couldn't drive to the hospital. I couldn't even stand up. I had internal bleeding and lost a lot of blood. I curled up in a fetal position on the floor. I didn't want sympathy from anyone, so I hid my illness and pain from everybody.

Omar had no idea how sick I was. I called him to come and help me. He lived about 20 minutes from me. I think he made it there in ten. Omar helped me into his car and drove me to Henry Ford Hospital, which was not far. I had more than one medical issue. Some of my pain was a result of a cyst on my ovary. The next morning, I had emergency surgery to remove the cyst. I lost half an ovary, and it was only the beginning of my hospital stay. Omar never left my side throughout this ordeal. My intestines and stomach were a mess. My colon was so infected and ulcerated that they couldn't operate on it right away. I would have to gain some weight and strength first. The pain medication only took the edge off my pain. It was constant pain every minute of the day. It was difficult for me to focus on reading my assignments and doing my homework. My head was spinning and foggy from all of the medication I was taking, but I knew I had to keep crawling. A few hours after the cyst removal surgery, I was lying in bed, half-awake, and heard my Dad calling to me. He was still in Lebanon at the time.

I said out loud, "Dad, are you here? Dad, why are you here?" He replied, "I've come to visit you and to comfort you." I woke up, started toward the bathroom, stopped, and thought, I'm sick. I just had surgery. I'm not supposed to get out of bed yet. I turned back, sat on the edge of the bed, and thought, oh my God, what did I do? My Dad just visited me for a moment, and for the first time, my pain was gone!

The nurse heard the noise and came running into my room and yelled, "What are you doing? You are not supposed to sit up or get out of bed!"

I told her I felt fine. The nurse said she didn't understand how I didn't have any pain. She helped me get back into my bed. As I lay there in bed, I thought I knew how it was possible. I didn't tell the nurse about the visit from Dad, but I think his visit helped relieve my pain. The next day, I had unbelievable pain again. I was so sore I couldn't move a muscle.

Eventually, I was discharged from the hospital and returned to my dental hygiene classes. Throughout my sickness and other roadblocks, I continued to crawl forward. I couldn't quit now.

Another unexpected roadblock surfaced while I was attending WCCC. Cases of the HIV virus began to spread in the inner-cities, and the spread was believed to be through contact with blood from an infected person. This fear spread among the dental community, and especially with students studying to enter the dental field. Rumors began to circulate among the student body about changing their course of study. Certainly, contact with blood would be a great risk as a dental hygienist. My close friends left the dental hygiene program and switched to an Associate of Science program. I joined my friends on their new course of study. I became afraid because all of my friends were terrified. I knew they were street smart and knew more than I did.

In May 1989, I graduated from Wayne County Community College with an Associate of Science degree. This was a big deal for me. It was a milestone in my quest for higher education. My friends and I went to enroll at Wayne State University after graduating from WCCC. The consular looked at my background in caring for elderly people, and recommended that I apply at Spring Arbor University. Spring Arbor had a campus on Outer Drive, in West Dearborn. I took his advice and talked to admissions at the Dearborn campus. It seemed like a nice, safe area.

I knew that having an Associate in Science degree would not get me very far in life. I decided I needed a bachelor's degree in business. Spring Arbor University accepted me into its business curriculum, so I went back to school to finish my goal of graduating with a bachelor's degree. My classes were all in the evening, so I was able to finish my chores during the day. The elderly lady I lived with waited up every night until I got home to make sure I was safe, which was typically around 11:30 p.m.

One day, I was so sick, I felt like I was about to die. An emergency room would have been the most logical place for me to head to next, but I couldn't let this hold me back. I drove to my class instead of the emergency room. I knew that missing a class would put me behind, and it would be hard to catch up. I had to work very hard every day if I wanted to make it. One of my teachers, Suzanne, looked at me when I entered her room and said, "Amira, your face is pale. You look sick. What's wrong with you?" I said, "I have a cold, and my stomach is hurting me." I was very sick; I could barely breathe.

She came closer to me and put her hand on my forehead and said, "Oh my God, I think you have a high fever. You better go see a doctor right away. I want you to go home now. I don't want you to stay in class."

I begged, "Please! I can't go home. I must study so I can pass the test. I don't want to fail, you know. It is a huge deal to me."

She replied, "No, you won't fail because you're sick. I promise you, I will help you." And then she repeated in a sterner voice, "I don't want you to stay in my class. I want you to leave before you make others sick. Amira, you look like you are dying. I'll ask your friend to take notes for you until you feel better." Suzanne promised to help me out with whatever I missed in class. She was very helpful to me.

I was pale and weak. I didn't argue with the teacher any further. It was easy to see that something was seriously wrong with me. It was as if I was saying "goodbye "to the world.

Then she said, "Is there something else going on in your life?" I replied, "Yes, there is. I divorced my husband. I am overwhelmed with emotion, and now I am sick. I feel depressed and scared about my life. I cry every day about what's going on in my life." She said not to worry about school. She said, "Take one day at a time. The things in your life you are going through now will pass. Go and see a doctor."

I did as she told me - I went to see a doctor. He knew right away that I had a severe case of bronchitis and suggested I stay at home for about a week until my fever was gone, and I felt well enough to return to school. He prescribed some antibiotics and told me to take my medicine and drink lots of water and stay in bed. I asked my sister, Suead, to help me with chores I couldn't do. I was so blessed to have a sister who supported me when I needed it. It helped me get through this toughest of times. I don't know if I could have continued crawling on my highway without her help along the way.

It had only been about five months since our divorce was final, and I was still hurting from the stress that I went through. I kept the burden all to myself. I finally told my Dad I was no longer married to Omar. He was shocked and saddened. We don't believe in divorce in my culture. It was shameful in Lebanon to separate and divorce. He said if he knew I was going to get a divorce, he wouldn't have allowed it to happen. I just kept crawling on the road to my goals, going to school and working.

In January 1991, I completed my bachelor's degree in the management of human resources at Spring Arbor University. Omar, his mom, Suead and her husband, Afif, came to the graduation ceremony. I was so proud of myself. I accomplished what I wanted to do after all the struggling. After I got my degree, I wondered what I would do next. Graduating from college was a lifelong dream that never left me through all of the perils along the way. But now what was I going to do with my life?

I enjoyed my work as a companion for older people until I graduated from college. The people liked me very much because they felt safe around me. I was honest with them. I created many activities to use, which made them feel good. I felt so good to be able to lift their spirits, especially people with dementia and other emotional issues. Omar suggested, "You are very good with elderly people. You probably would do very well working at a nursing home. I think you have a special talent."

Continuing My Journey on the Highway

My career path, using Activities for residents with Alzheimer's Disease began when I was hired as an Activities Director at the Courtyard Manor Nursing Home upon graduating from Spring Arbor University. When the manager took me on a tour of the facility, I was amazed and scared. Two hundred fifty people in three buildings were an immense responsibility for me. The manager expected me to develop an activities program without help from anyone. The manager liked me very much, especially my positive and energetic attitude. She could tell I really wanted this job. I accepted the position. I worked intensely hard to make it a successful program. A bachelor's degree, combined with my experiences as a caregiver and companion to the elderly, paid off. This job was my opportunity to show how much I loved working with older people and how I could manage the challenges associated with Alzheimer's.

Many residents were diagnosed with dementia. Dementia is about memory loss. I found my techniques could help them regain some of their lost memory. Knowing their past experiences, I customized the activities to their history and rekindled lost memories. I also introduced them to new activities that, with enough repetition, they eventually remembered. When they enjoyed a new activity, they recalled it. As their memory improved, they were amazed and proud of their accomplishments.

Omar was so impressed with how I used activities to enhance the well-being of so many residents that he encouraged me to document everything I accomplished at the nursing home. Omar was behind me 100% in my quest to fulfill my dreams. He was amazed at how my activities were helping people feel better, even when they had Alzheimer's.

My husband was so proud of me for taking on such a big job. I was responsible for purchasing activity supplies for the entire facility with just $200 per month. I needed to get resourceful, so I began creating my activities. Most of my supplies for my activities came from the Dollar Store and hardware store. Everyone seemed to like my creative activities better than ordinary games. Holidays were stressful times for me. It was a time of high anxiety to prepare for celebrations and emotions from family visits. Sometimes I would tell Omar, "This is too much work for me. I can't handle this without help." They promised to hire an assistant, but this never materialized. Omar volunteered to help me decorate for Christmas and other occasions because it was just too much for one person to handle.

Amira the Author and Teacher

I was always excited to return home and tell Omar about an exciting new activity I came up with, and how well it worked with some of the residents. Omar said to me, "From what I've read, people with severe dementia can't regain lost memories because Alzheimer's destroyed the brain cells." I insisted it was possible because I had heard it with my ears and seen it with my eyes. Each activity may not work with everyone, so I used the ones that did help. Everyone was unique and needed customized activities.

Omar suggested if it's true that I am restoring memories with residents, and I could prove it, I needed to share it with the rest of the world. "Amira, you need to take notes of what activities work and how to do them. Also, document the ones that didn't work. It is amazing to hear how you help so many people with dementia. You have a special skill. What is it that you do differently than other caregivers? Others need to know your techniques and learn your skills. You can help the residents you're working with, but if you write a book describing what you've learned, you can help many more people."

Writing a book sounded good, but I had no clue where I would begin. Omar encouraged me to take detailed notes and start making videos of my before and after activity treatments. Of course, I would need signed approval from family members and staff to pursue my project. Everyone was supportive of documenting my achievements. I started to take many detailed notes. I continued to write down what was working and what was not working for the next two years.

As I was collecting the information, we began organizing the notes into chapters and writing my first book, and in 1999, I published "Healing the Wounds of Alzheimer's Disease." It captured many of the activities and techniques I had used over the past few years. The book explained what Alzheimer's was about and included many activities, techniques, and real-life examples.

My experiences and education prepared me to give workshops about my creative actives and unique techniques to unlock clouded memories. Symptoms of dementia, in many cases, can be reversed, or the progression slowed down. The success I experienced was ground-breaking in the field of treating people with dementia.

As soon as I had 2,000 hours of experience, combined with a Bachelor's degree, I would meet the qualifications to become a Certified Activities Consultant. I continued working many hours with the residents, the staff, and the caregivers. The certification would give me recognition and respect by my peers. Being certified became a requirement to qualify as an Activity Director. Courtyard Manor gave me a letter stating I worked as an Activity Director for two years. I became certified as an activities consultant (ACC) by the National Certification Council of Activity Professionals (NCCAP), the highest level of certification available.

Teaching Caregivers and Students

I began to do presentations at nearby facilities, and, eventually, facilities in other states and Canada invited me to present at their events.

With my certification in hand, I interviewed to teach at a local college. I presented my proposal to Henry Ford Community College to teach caregivers, nurses, and activity professionals. They accepted me to teach a night school class. I taught for about five years. I also gave a presentation at Madonna University to their gerontology students.

I began traveling all over the country with Omar to train nurses, social workers, caregivers, and other activities professionals. I traveled from California to New York, and everywhere in between. In 2003, I published another book titled "ABC's of Activities for Alzheimer's." In addition to the book, I produced a one hour and ten minute video so caregivers could learn by watching how I introduced activities. I thought it would be suitable for people who didn't enjoy reading. Seeing is believing. The DVD took a year to complete. This DVD, "ABC's of Activities for Alzheimer's" became very popular among caregivers because it was created by someone who understood what was happening in their lives. I knew first-hand how difficult it was to take care of people with dementia.

I demonstrated and explained the activities included in my book. My book wasn't only 1,001 activities. There were already books for that. My book explained the details of what worked for me. My focus was on the techniques that made them successful. I knew my methods worked because I had helped hundreds, maybe thousands of people improve their quality of life.

Before Mom died, I told her, "I'm going to put you in a video."

"Really? I'm going to be in your video?" she asked.

"Yes, Mom." She was so excited, and so was I, but she didn't live long enough to see it completed. However, her picture is in my books and video.

I always enjoyed watching The Oprah Show, and occasionally seeing her friend, Steadman Graham on her talk show. I felt proud at one convention when I was presenting in the room adjacent to the place where Steadman Graham was presenting.

My session ended at the same time his did, so I grasped the chance to meet him. When I told him that I was presenting next door, he saw my book "Activity Techniques That Heal the Wounds of Alzheimer's" I had clasped in my hand. He agreed to sign my book. I felt so important, presenting next to a celebrity. He asked if I could send him a copy. I reached in my briefcase and gave him a new book I had carried with me.

Dr. Maya Angelou, an American poet, memoirist, actress and respected pioneer and activist for civil rights, presented in another room near mine. I had the opportunity to meet her after listening to her moving presentation. I will never forget the compassionate and humble story of her highway to success. It touched my heart when I reflected on my own struggles.

On one occasion, there were too many boxes and supplies to ship or fly, so we drove for 36 hrs. to St. John's, Canada so I could give a 3-day presentation. It was the middle of winter. Omar drove to St. Johns and back, in blinding snow, to support me.

I continued to learn more with every resident or client I met. In 2011, I published an updated book, with many new activities, titled, "Therapeutic Activities for Persons with Dementia." In 2014, I published my latest activities book titled "Amazing Activities for Low Function Abilities and Caregiver Guide," with updated information about Alzheimer's Disease and included many more creative activities and resources. I always believed if you know something that can benefit others, or make their road easier to travel, you should share it with them.

Although social media discussed Alzheimer's Disease, I could not find any discussions about how to improve memory function. The audience for my books was limited to caregivers for someone with dementia, and further limited to those who cared enough to seek out help for their loved one. Caregivers were already aware there is no cure for Alzheimer's and it is a degenerating disease. They also knew their care would not be necessary for a long time. Why should they do anything for their loved ones? Reports suggest that nothing can stop the decline of Alzheimer's. No studies had been done that would show help is available to help delay the progression and make their final journey so much happier. I could make them feel better. Most accepted the fate of living through the slippery slope of declining memory.

I have many amazing stories in my book. Here is one: A man and his wife were in the same facility, The Henry Ford Village. She had Alzheimer's, and her husband was dying from a complication of a severe liver problem. She was angry at him, and they didn't get along. She would ask me over and over, "What am I going to do about money when my husband dies?"

I knew it would make her feel better if she had answers to those questions. So I put them together in the same room. She was sitting on the side of her bed, and her husband was lying down in his hospital bed. She did not want to talk to him at all. I sat in a chair between them and pulled their beds as close as I could. I spoke to each of them and negotiated between them, back and forth. I asked him to hold her hand, and her to hold his. I told her that her husband had something he wanted to say to her. I held each of their hands and pulled them together. They held hands as I continued to talk with them.

I said, "You told me you love your wife. I want you to tell her you do love her."

"I love you, honey," he said.

She responded with, "I love you, too."

Then, I said, "Tell her about the money you have for her."

He said, "I have a ton of money for you and the kids. You won't have to worry about money if I die."

She replied, "Oh, I did worry so much, but I was afraid to ask you about money. I feel better now." All it took to relieve her anger was to resolve what bothered her. I asked them to hug each other. I helped her to his bedside, and they embraced for a long hug and a kiss. The next day, he died peacefully. Real stories like this are in my activities book. My confidence and self-esteem were growing with each success in my life. My dreams were being fulfilled one at a time.

Nada comes to America

My next big dream was to have my younger sister, Nada, with me in America. Nada had many friends in Lebanon and a respected job as a nurse. She was happily married to Ali Abi Haidar, and had two beautiful daughters, Amira who was six years old and Aya was three. I never thought that she would visit America. Her life was in Lebanon.

One day, in 1997, I heard that Nada and her family were coming to America. I was in absolute disbelief. Could it be true? I insisted she would live with us in America. I jumped and frolicked around the house when I heard the good news. Omar asked what was going on. Before I could calm down enough to answer him, I was crying. Again, he asked what's wrong. As I wiped away my tears of joy, I replied, "Nothing's wrong. My sister, Nada, is coming to America to live, and she will stay with us."

We met her and her family at the airport, and I will never forget the exuberant feeling that came over me when I saw them come through the security door. Nada was carrying her youngest daughter, Aya, in her arms, and Amira was hanging on to her. Ali had a big smile and a peaceful face. I was beside myself with joy.

Nada and her family stayed with us for some time while they looked for a house to rent in Dearborn. Dearborn has a predominately Middle Eastern population. Ali got a job in a meat market and began saving money to buy a home. Once he became acclimated to his new environment, Ali worked for a few years until he started his own landscaping company. Eventually, they bought a beautiful home in Dearborn.

It was wonderful to have my Mom, two sisters and their families together again. For the next several years, we took care of my Mom's health and spent quality time as a real family. This is how I always thought a family should be. I loved my Mom so much that I wanted to keep her to myself. But, of course, I knew I had to share her with my sisters. Even when my Mom stayed at Nada or Suead's house, I visited her as much as I could. Our family grew closer with my Mom's presence. She was like the glue that held us together and repaired the cracks that occurred. I wanted to spend as much time with her as I possibly could. My Mom's health began to worsen in her later years, and the painful truth was that she wouldn't be with us forever.

Myself, Nada, My Mom, and Suead

Chapter 16
Passing of My Parents

One morning, I got up at 5:00 am to go to the Jewish Community Center. I went to Mom's room and said, "Mom, I'm leaving to go exercise now." She said, "Okay, God bless you."

When I returned home, I went into her room, and Mom asked, "I'm glad you're back, but who is the person with you?"

"No one," I said. "I am by myself. What person are you talking about?"

"There is a beautiful lady with you, with a long, white dress, walking beside you."

"There is no one with me." I looked at her and said, "Oh my God, Mom, you're getting confused. You see things that aren't there."

"No, I'm not confused, I know I see a woman with you. Can't you see her walking with you?"

She repeated it several times. I was very concerned my Mom was losing her mind and/or hallucinating. I took Mom to see a psychiatrist at St. Mary's Hospital, where she was receiving dialysis treatment. I told the doctor, "My Mom might be hallucinating. She told me she saw a woman next to me and described what she looked like in great detail."

The doctor spoke and understood Arabic well so Mom could answer questions clearly, in her native language. Mom confessed she had seen this woman with me many times. Her description was the same each time. She looked very peaceful and kind. The woman may have been a Guardian Angel.

The doctor said, "Well, I'll test her, and we'll see what's going on." He asked her some questions like: "Do you know what year this is? Can you tell me what time it is now? Do you know where you are right now? Do you know who the president is?" He then continued talking with her to observe her cognitive ability.

Mom was sharp and answered all of the questions correctly. He was amazed by her knowledge and ability to articulate the answers clearly.

Mom asked, "Doctor, can I ask you a question?" He replied, "Yes, please ask."

"What do you think...Am I out-of-it, or with it?" The doctor laughed and said, "You're not out-of-it! I think you are smarter than I am!"

I thought that possibly her medication was causing her to hallucinate. Then I began to rethink my rational explanation. Was my Mom seeing an Angel walking beside me? It was the only other answer to her visions. After I saw with my own eyes and ears that she had all her mental faculties. I believed she saw visions that were real. I wasn't sure what the visions meant, but I believed they were real and had a significant meaning.

Passing of My Mom

A few weeks later, in late May 2001, I was planning to attend a wedding. Omar's nephew, Cooper, was getting married on Grosse Isle. It was about an hour and fifteen drive from our house, so I expected to be coming home late. Earlier in the day, I took my Mom to get her dialysis treatment at St. Mary's Hospital. Suead said she would pick her up after the dialysis treatment. Mom was now very sick. She had many problems with her health, but she always stayed positive.

Before we left for the hospital, I had a long talk with my Mom. I explained that this wedding was important to Omar. All of his family and close friends would be there for the wedding party. She said to me, "I don't want you to go to the wedding." I was surprised because she never objected to me going anywhere before.

"Why?" I asked.

She said, "I feel like you should be with me today."

At that point, I was upset, but I didn't listen to her. I was going to the wedding and Suead would pick her up from the hospital. My decision was firm. Mom was upset and her face was sad.

I brought watermelon pieces for my Mom and me to share in the car on the way to the hospital. Mom loved watermelon, and I offered her some from my bowl. She continued to stare out the side window, I looked at her and asked, "Mom, do you want watermelon?"

"No," she said.

"Why not?"

She answered, "Because I just don't. I don't want you to go to the wedding."

I insisted that I was going. It was unusual for my Mom to keep to herself on the way to the hospital. The trip was always a happy time for us to talk and laugh. But this day was different. My Mom was silent and oblivious to any of my gestures. Her face was not the usual smile. It was a sad face. Maybe she knew something I didn't know about this day.

When I arrived at the hospital, I told the nurse, "Please take care of my Mom. My sister, Suead, will pick her up."

As I left the hospital, I told her not to worry, that Suead would pick her up and take her home. This time, I wouldn't be able to pick her up from her treatment. Again, she didn't respond to what I told her. She just tilted her head toward her hand and kept looking up at me with a sad look on her face.

We went to the wedding, and at 5 pm, I reminded Suead it was time for her to go to the hospital to pick up Mom.

At about 5:30, I called Suead and asked, "Where is Mom?" She said, "She's at home."

She said Sarah picked her grandmother up from the hospital and took her back home. Sarah stayed with her for about 30 minutes while Mom cooked some eggs for herself.

Later that evening, while the party was just getting into full swing, I felt I needed to call my Mom. I wasn't sure why it felt urgent, but something told me to call her. I called Mom's number, but she didn't answer the phone. I called her again. But again, no answer. I then called my sister, Suead, and asked if she knew why Mom didn't answer the phone. She did not know either. I panicked and called my neighbor. "Flo, can you please go to my house and check on my Mom? She is not answering the phone. The back door is unlocked." I stayed on the phone while Flo checked on my Mom. Flo returned to the phone and said, "Please give the phone to Omar. You are too upset to talk. Please calm down." I handed my cell phone to Omar. She had found Mom lying in her bed with her eyes closed. She had a peaceful look on her face, and Flo thought she was sleeping. She put her hand on Mom's face. It was cold. Flo told Omar the sad news. Omar asked her again, "What did you say?" Flo said, "I think she is dead."

Omar told me, "We are leaving now." Omar was shaking, and said to Flo, "We are about an hour away. Can you please call the police?"

I had a feeling my Mom wasn't there. I asked Omar, "What's wrong?" I lost it. I couldn't talk anymore.

Omar drove straight home. I was going crazy all the way there. I was upset and driving Omar crazy. I was trying to get him to drive faster, but he said he could not drive any faster, or the police would stop us and give us a speeding ticket. I kept yelling and screaming. When we got home, I saw the police and EMS in our driveway. I tried to go to my Mom but the police wouldn't allow me in her room until they finished their job, I think it took about 15 minutes, but it felt like we waited a day. I peeked around the officer standing in the doorway to see her in her bed. She had a pleasant look on her face, and a glow that was the most peaceful look I can ever imagine in my life. She had neatly pulled up the blanket, and the TV was on her favorite channel. My Mom didn't look dead to me, she looked like an Angel lying there, resting with her eyes closed.

The police finally let me see my Mom. They told me she had been dead for an hour and a half. They were now ready to take her. "I don't want her to go!" I begged. One of the EMS men looked at me and said, "Ma'am, she has to go now."

Wiping away my tears, I pleaded, "The rest of my family is on their way. Can't we wait until they get here?" He agreed. My family members came, but they were all crying and praying, and we couldn't even talk. I was yelling and screaming and wanting to fight. I was angry she left me without saying goodbye. I stood over my Mom and kept shouting, "Why did you leave me without telling me you were going?" Omar tried to calm me by assuring me that "I'm sure if she knew, she would have told you." Nothing could calm me down. I needed to get my emotions out. If I didn't, I think I would have exploded. I was crying hysterically, and I didn't know how to stop.

My Mom's sudden death was a shock to all of us. We knew she had health issues, but no one was prepared for her to go so quickly, without warning. Maybe it was a blessing for her to die peacefully. If I had been there to see her dying, I don't think I could have handled it well. Mom was afraid of dying. She exercised, went for daily walks, and took her medicine so she could live longer. Dying in her sleep, without suffering, was the least fearful way for her to pass on. We all stayed until they covered her body and put her in the EMS van. No one was allowed to follow them, so we all went to Suead's house in Northville.

While sitting on the white leather couch at my sister's house, I saw a ball of blue and purple light travel from my head, down my chest, across my lap, down past my toes, and then it disappeared. I screamed to everyone, "Do you see that light? Do you see that blue light?" No one saw it but me. I believe it may have been my Mom's spirit. We all talked, cried, and prayed into the night.

I didn't want to go back to our house that night. I didn't want to believe my Mom was no longer there. My sister, Nada, asked us to stay at her house in Dearborn. We stayed up most of the night talking and praying. We were planning to get up early to go to the funeral home. I didn't sleep at all. I just lay there, in bed, with my eyes open. As I laid quietly, I saw a beautiful butterfly flying around in the room. It was flying in a circle as if it was outside, frolicking in the sunshine. I called Nada to ask if she knew that a butterfly was in her house. She said she had never seen one inside before.

The next morning, my sisters and I went to the funeral home to wash my Mom and prepare her for the funeral. When the mortician slid her out to give us access to her body, I began talking to her again, asking her why she left me so fast. They moved my Mom to a private room where we could wash her. This was the last caring thing I could do for my Mom.

After we finished taking care of my Mom, Suead and I went into the bathroom. As soon as we closed the door behind us, I heard a rattling and clanking noise in the room with me. I asked Suead if she heard the same noises. She said, "Oh my God, is something making a noise in here? Sister, what do you think it is?" I said, "Somebody is with me right here." "I don't see anything," Suead replied. We got out of there as soon as we could.

I went back and stood alongside my Mom's casket, and started yelling at her again. I was still furious about her dying. I know it wasn't a rational question, but it was an overpowering emotion. I was out of control.

"Why did you do this to me?" I demanded. I didn't understand it.

My Mom's Final Trip to Lebanon

We needed to prepare to take my Mom to Lebanon, where she wished to be buried. Issam came from Oregon. He loved my Mom so much, and he was just as upset as I about her death. We were all at Nada's house in Dearborn. Omar and I were sitting together, and again I saw a butterfly. I didn't know how the butterfly got into the house. I didn't know why, but it came directly to me.

The following day, we went to the funeral home to fill out the papers for her body to be transported to Lebanon. We then went back to our home in West Bloomfield. As we entered the house, the phone started to ring. It kept ringing again and again, maybe ten times. It had never rung like that before. Slowly I picked up the receiver and said, "Hello?"

The voice said, "I hope your mom is feeling better."

I did not recognize the voice. I asked, "What did you say?" She hung up. I didn't recognize the phone number or the voice heard. I knew all of her nurses' voices and phone numbers. I was baffled as to why a stranger would ask about my Mom.

Omar and I went back to the funeral home to join the other family members. We gathered to share our feelings of shock and grief. We sat and talked for some time. I felt close to my Mom in spirit. Everything we talked about revolved around her, all of the joy we shared when she was alive. Each of us had a story to tell. God, I missed her.

The next day, everything was arranged for our trip to Lebanon. We all arrived at the funeral home to take my Mom to the airport. She had been packaged into a shipping box that looked like another piece of baggage. It made my heart hurt to know that this would be her final trip. She should be sitting with us, not dead in a shipping box. I had crazy thoughts like she can't breathe inside that box. It's dark and cold inside. I wanted to comfort and tell her that everything will be alright. Everything was not okay. My Mom was gone. We followed the slow-moving hearse to the airport where the baggage handlers picked her up. We rushed to the gate where my sisters and I would be departing. We stared out through the plane's window as they loaded the baggage into the baggage bay, trying to get a glimpse of our precious Mom loaded into the plane. We spotted the box that contained her body.

I wanted them to be gentle with her, but they were not. I wanted to yell at them to be careful, it's my Mom in that box, but I couldn't. Once again, my heart started pounding and aching. This time the pain was even more profound. I could no longer help her. No more daily trips with me to the hospital, no more frequent trips to buy food, no more feeding the swan that came to visit her on our deck. No more walks to the hidden blackberry bush, around the corner, to bring Omar his favorite fruit and no more Kit-Kats from her. All of these thoughts raced through my mind as I saw her loaded into the cargo bay.

When we arrived at the airport in Beirut, Lebanon, we were met by my brother, Adnan, his family, and many relatives and friends. It looked like at least 1,000 people were waiting for us to arrive. I knew my Mom had made many friends in Lebanon, but I had never seen them all gathered in one place before. We took her body to my Dad's house, where family and friends packed into his home. Dad didn't show any emotion to indicate he felt sorry for her or that he grieved over her passing. He was now married to a second wife much younger than my Mom. He stood next to his new wife the whole time, instead of next to my Mom's casket. I hated her so much because she took my Dad away from my Mom and our family. Most of his money and property went to his new wife. My Mom never received anything from him after he remarried. My Mom never said anything negative about my Dad, and never allowed anyone of us to speak with disrespect about him. She cared about him until the day she died. But in my opinion, he didn't deserve the respect he demanded from others.

The next day, we gathered around my Mom's casket for the last time. There were about 1,000 people in attendance. Everyone who knew my Mom loved her. She was buried in our family cemetery plot, just behind the fruit trees, next to the garden that we worked so hard on. The cemetery plot next to hers was prepared for my Dad. He would be next to my Mom in his final resting place.

We stayed in Lebanon for a week before coming back home. I was so depressed that I was seeing darkness all the time, and when the sun was shining, a dense fog shrouded the sun. My depression was very severe. I continued to have many visions and messages from my Mom after she died. On one occasion, I was in a tall building looking out an open window when I heard my Mom call my name. She was on the ground, looking up at me. I was going to jump to her from the highest floor of the building to see her. She said, "No, Amira, I will come up to get you." She flew up and took me with her. We flew around the sky with her holding my hand the entire time.

I said, "Mama! Are you really here? How are you? I miss you so much! Why did you do this to me? What happened to you? Where did you go?"

She never answered, but I kept asking questions. Mom just took my hand and pulled me through the emotional hardship I was experiencing.

Then I said to her, "Tell me what is going on up there? Are you happy? Are you okay?"

She said, "Do not ask me questions. I cannot tell you anything. I cannot answer any of your questions. But one thing I want to tell you, there is a God."

"Tell me more, Mama, tell me more!"

But then, she left me all by myself. My experience that seemed so real was all a dream. When I opened my eyes, it was a beautiful morning and there was a warm, comforting feeling all over my body. I wondered if this is how my Mom would visit me, in my dreams.

When we returned to our home in West Bloomfield, I tried to keep in contact with Mom by going into her room and talking to her. I would sit on her chair and say, "Mama, if you are here, please talk to me. Or if you don't want to speak, just do something. I just want to feel you."

The chandelier in her room got my attention when I saw it move. That was when I said to myself, "I know you are here, Mama. But why did you go?" I was talking to her as if she was still alive. I was still angry about her death.

I asked Suead, who was waiting in the kitchen, just outside Mom's room, "Do you know that Mama is around? I just talked to her."

My sister looked at me as if she was saying, yes, I believe you. But I had a feeling she thought I was hallucinating from the depression and grieving that I was going through.

I told her, "Yes, it's true."

"What are you talking about?" she asked.

"I talked with Mom. I asked her to give me a sign that she was with me, and she moved the chandelier. I will ask her to do it again."

We went to her room, but I did not let Suead come in. I made her stand outside her door. I wanted it to be just me and Mom in the room.

I asked again, "Mama, if you're here, can you move the chandelier?"

I saw the chandelier move again, and I said, "Sis, did you see it move?"

"I'm not sure." Suead said.

"Come here! Look closer!" I said.

"Maybe a little bit, I don't know," she said.

I said, "I can see it moving! I can see it!" I was excited to see a sign from my Mom. I asked again if she could see it move. Suead insisted she could not. I saw what I saw, but I don't think Suead saw it. I believe that Mom intended her message to be just for me. It made me feel special.

It was about a year after my Mom passed that I was able to move anything in her room. I knew my Dad was applying for a visa to visit America, and he would ask to stay with me. Until then, everything was just as she left it. Even her coffee cup and coffee pot were not touched. The bed and the blanket were still intact. I never touched anything in her room and did not let anyone else enter her room. Even my sisters were not allowed to go in there, and I told them that they could only see from two steps back from the doorway. They were getting annoyed with me, but I meant business.

I had taken care of her for seven years. I had a family who was willing to help me with my Mom, but she wanted to be with me and Omar, whom she loved very much. Omar recalled often times when he was on the computer late at night, and she used to give him a donut from the refrigerator. When she passed, Omar stopped using the computer for a while. When he finally got back on the computer, something strange happened. He said, as he was focusing on his computer, he felt a tap on his shoulder. There was no one there, but he felt a familiar tap on his shoulder. My mother wasn't there to give him the donut any longer, but the tap on the shoulder was still there.

After my Mom had passed, all of my brothers and sisters remained very angry with my Dad. Other relatives and even our neighbors, anyone who knew my Mom, hated my Dad. Mom was an angel. I couldn't get rid of the haunting question, "What did you do, Dad? You could never find a better woman than Mom." Dad married another woman because he always wanted someone to be with him. He wanted a companion he could have fun with. That was how my Dad was. I thought I would never want to see him again.

Dad contacted us about one year after Mom's death. He said that his visa had been approved, and he was coming to America the following week. As angry as I was with him, I didn't have the heart to say no. I simply replied, "Okay. You are welcome to come, Dad."

Inside my head, my mind screamed, "What the hell are you doing, coming here? How rude you are! You're coming here after my Mom's death, and you never came to see her when she was around? You didn't come to visit when she asked you to? And now that she is gone, you're coming to visit us and sleep in her empty room? We don't need your love, we don't need your help, and we don't need you!"

Two days before Dad arrived, I cried so hard. I stayed up until 2:00 a.m. and then kept waking up, crying, until my alarm clock sounded at 6:00 a.m. How could I accept my Dad in my house and put him in my Mom's room, of all places, especially since he didn't show her any love? I had no option, since it was the only room available. I had to clean her room out for him to stay with us. The thought of letting him sleep on the same bed that my Mom slept in was haunting me. I regretted that I agreed to let my Dad stay with us.

I began preparing her room for my Dad's arrival. It was difficult to clean her room, knowing she was gone, and that she was the last one to touch her things. When I began cleaning out her room, I discovered my tape recorder, the one that I practiced my presentations with. It was alongside her bed. I didn't understand how it got there. I knew Mom wouldn't know how to use it because it was digital, and not easy to use. I thought maybe I accidently left it there, so I put it back in the drawer where I always kept it.

I placed her items neatly on her bed, and gazed at them for a while. Tears flowed down my cheeks, blurring my vision as I moved her belongings. Until now, I hadn't allowed anyone to go into her room. I cried and talked with my Mom as I moved one item at a time. As I was grieving and picking up her Quran and touching her clothing that she had neatly arranged in her closet, I heard my Mom say to me, very clearly, "Amira, it's okay. Let it be. It's okay."

"What, Mama?" I asked out loud.

She repeated, "It's okay." I felt she was giving me permission to clean the room and she was not upset with me. Preparing my Mom's room for Dad's visit with her permission made it much easier for me to swallow. Before I heard her sweet voice of approval, I was only doing it because I had to.

I was leaving her room to go to the bathroom across from my Mom's bedroom. I looked behind me and called out, "Mama! Mama!" Following me out of her room was a wispy cloud in the shape of a large teardrop which trailed off at the bottom. It was about half the size of my body and got bigger and thicker as it turned toward the kitchen. I kept looking in amazement until it disappeared through the refrigerator.

I screamed, "Oh my God, Oh my God!" I told Omar about the white cloud. He knew how close I was to my Mom, and he believed she was communicating that she was here with me, and the cloud was a way to validate her presence. My Mom's favorite snack foods were Kit-Kat candy bars and plain donuts (the donuts she gave Omar while he was working late on his computer each night.) She kept them in the same refrigerator that the white cloud passed through. Maybe she was saying, "Don't forget my favorite snacks in the refrigerator."

Several months later, I took the voice recorder out of my drawer to use it. I pressed play to see where I left off. I was in disbelief to hear my Mom's sweet voice on the recorder. The real surprise was that Mom learned how to use it. It was a tiny recorder, not much larger than a pack of gum. In her later years, my Mom developed arthritis and had stiff joints and limited use of her fingers. It was difficult even for me to use these little recording devices. How in the world did she learn to operate this thing? She couldn't read the instructions, so we don't know how she did it, or even when. It seemed as though it was nothing less than a miracle.

The message she left was healing for me. Until then, I thought she died without saying goodbye. I found out how wrong I was. She said goodbye in her way when she was alive and found a way to do it. She left a parting message on the tape recorder. She said, "When I'm gone, you kids take care of each other and know that I will be watching over you after I pass." Within the message, she sang a religious song to me. There were some talks about her sisters. She also said she knew she was going to die soon.

On the recording, Mom said, "I love you children, and when I am not here, don't think I am not with you. I am watching over you to take care of you. I love all of you for everything that you have done for me." Mom was grateful for life and grateful for everything we gave back to her until her last breath. We miss you so much Mom!

Dad Comes to America

In 2002, one year after my Mom died, my Dad came to America to visit us. He was 79 years old when he came. He went through many difficulties in his life when Mom was often sick. Eventually, he set out to make a new life and found a younger woman who could satisfy his ego and manly desires. Leaving my Mom for another woman was very troubling to me. My Mom waited on him hand and foot while they were married. She served him with every ounce of her energy, even when she was very sick, and he left her!

Mom never talked negatively about my Dad. She always spoke highly about anything he did and defended him if anyone else spoke otherwise about him. This was her reward for dedicating her life to him?

We welcomed our Dad when he arrived at the airport. About 15 family members were there to greet him. We brought him to our home in West Bloomfield to stay with us. When he came into our home, he seemed happy and relaxed. I was going to tell him that the room he would be staying in had been an office, but when I looked at him, I couldn't hide the truth, just to protect his feelings.

When we took his bags into Mom's room, I asked my Dad, "Do you know that you will be sleeping in my Mom's bedroom?"

He replied, very calmly, "Oh!" He was unemotional and matter of fact about her passing. Dad didn't have anything to say.

I didn't say much to him that day either. He was exhausted from the trip, and I didn't want to unload all my pent-up negative feelings on his first day in America.

The next day, I asked my Dad, "Why did you do this to my Mom? Why did you get married to another woman?" I asked him, "Are you happy with your life?" He stared straight into my eyes and said, "No, to be honest with you. I am miserable." I asked him, "Did you love my mom enough?" He said, "It felt like it was enough for her. Your Mom treated me with respect and kindness. Even when I was angry, spewed out angry words and used vulgar language, and even when I hit her, she still smiled. That's why I loved your Mom. She had so much kindness, love, and forgiveness." He felt guilty from it all, and said, "If I could turn the clock back 15 years, I would. I would do better, but I can't change what I've already done."

A few days later, Omar and I took my Dad to visit my sister, Suead, and her husband, Afif. We were all relaxing and having family conversation as my sister prepared to serve dinner. Out of the blue, I asked my Dad if he wanted to know how I killed the sheep.

"Did you kill the sheep?" he asked, genuinely surprised.

"Yes, I did," I said.

He asked, "How did you kill the sheep?"

"Well..." I started. "You asked me to care for her. Make sure she had enough food. Make sure she had enough water. And if I didn't do that, I would get in trouble. When she wouldn't drink water, I kicked her on the stomach and she died."

"Really?" he scratched his head.

"What are you going to do now?" I said nervously. The fear from that time came back.

"Well, I can't do anything about it," he laughed. "You didn't tell me the truth."

"Of course," I said. "You would have killed me at that time. You would have never let me live."

"I wouldn't do that to you," he laughed again.

Then my brother-in-law, Afif, asked my Dad, "How come you didn't hurt her or punish her for that?"

Dad thought about it for a minute. Then he stretched back in the chair he was sitting in and smiled. "She wrote me a good letter with so much love. 'I missed you, Dad.' Her letter melted my heart, and I didn't want to hurt her."

Dad had planned to stay in America for one month. He called his wife, Ensaf, every day and cried because he missed her. He couldn't take being away from her for that long, so he returned to Lebanon after only a two-week stay.

Our Final Visit to See My Dad in Lebanon

A few years after Dad's visit, Omar and I visited him in Lebanon, when Lubna was about nine years old. Omar and I were sitting outside on the porch, talking with Ensaf. Lubna seemed interested in teasing Omar by hitting him on the arm as she uttered loud grunting sounds. She kept tugging on his shirt sleeve.

She then tried to push Omar over the edge of the porch onto some rocks. Fortunately, Omar was also strong and stood his ground. Dad grabbed the stick that was close to where he was sitting. As he raised his stick toward Lubna, Ensaf stepped in between Dad and Lubna. I jumped up to defend my husband. I gave her a sour face and screamed, "Don't do this to my husband!" I grabbed her arm and shook her. My eyes were very wide open. I must have scared her because she let go of him and went back into the house.

She smiled at us from inside the doorway as if nothing had happened and just stared at us with an unfocused look. She came back and kept reaching for Omar and pulling on his arm to come into the house. He turned the tables on her and began chasing her around the house as he grunted sounds to mimic hers. She found this very amusing and enjoyed escaping from his grasp. She kept running and laughing until she became exhausted and collapsed on the couch. He discovered that chasing Lubna around the house kept her mind occupied and burned off some of her excess energy. Lubna seemed to calm down after that.

Even with Ensaf around, my Dad did not feel safe. Ensaf continually had a hard time with her daughter's violent behavior. They tried putting her in a special institution, but the institution did not want her because it was too much risk for the staff and other residents. My Dad was trapped in his self-made hell. His only escape came in 2006.

My Dad Passes Away

My Dad died in 2006. When he died, it took a long time for him to pass. We don't know how long he suffered, but it wasn't quick. Adnan told me about his painful suffering. Ensaf called Adnan and with a very calm voice, said, "Your Dad is dying." My brother came to him during the last hours of his life. Ensaf did not take him to the hospital. Adnan took him, but he was pronounced dead when they arrived. It seemed that Dad's wife wanted him to die. She didn't try to help him when he was dying. I felt as though she was after his money. She fed him fried chicken and all greasy foods. Fatty foods were the kind that she liked for herself. When he passed, she became wealthy.

Adnan and his family attended his funeral. Adnan was the only child of his that attended. Even though I didn't like how my Dad treated us when we were growing up, I cried when I heard how he died. Good or bad...he was still my Dad, and I felt sorry for him. In some ways, I still miss him.

Chapter 17
The Car Accident

In June 2006, we had a severe car accident. I don't remember much about what happened that night. I was knocked unconscious after the first rollover. I remember Omar trying to kick his door open and yelling for help from a male bystander. Omar asked the stunned man to pull on the twisted door so Omar could pull me out. I was shocked when I saw what appeared to be smoke pouring from the hood. I screamed at Omar, "Are we going to burn to death? We're on fire! We're on fire! Oh my God, is this how my life will end?" Omar stayed calm and assured me the car was not on fire. It was steam coming from the radiator.

Omar's Account of the Event

We were looking forward to attending a Detroit Tigers baseball game. We were not much interested in baseball, but the tickets to the game were a gift from my employer, so we decided to go. It was an enjoyable event and nice to experience something different that evening. We were driving toward home at 10:30 pm. I was in the fast lane, going about 70 miles per hour. Four lanes over was a car swerving out of control. It spun from that lane, four lanes over, and hit me in the side. The impact turned my car around and flipped us over four times. We ended up landing on the wheels on the opposite side of the freeway, facing the wrong direction. Immediately, I saw that Amira was knocked out, and she had blood coming from her head.

I shook her and said, "Are you okay?"

She answered in a weak voice, "What happened?"

"Never mind what happened! Let's get the hell out of here!"

The car was steaming, beat up on all sides, and the windows were all broken out. The car was empty. The violent tumbling had thrown everything from our vehicle: the glovebox, center console, and everything in the back of our car was gone.

Earlier in the day, I removed a large, heavy laser printer from the back of the car before we left our house. While parked downtown at the game, I didn't want to tempt anyone to steal the printer. And luckily, I did, or else we both would be dead. The force of that large printer would have easily killed us.

The man in the car ahead of us came running back, looked in the window and yelled, "I can't believe anyone is alive in this car!"

I pleaded with him, "Never mind that! Can you please pull on that door so I can try and kick it open so we can get out of here?"

He pulled hard on the door, and I kicked it until it popped open. I pulled Amira over the center-console and out the open door. We sat on the grass alongside the road. EMS arrived and took us to the closest emergency room. There were no broken or fractured bones, but cuts and bruises covered our bodies. Our ears were ringing and filled with chunks of crumpled glass. Amira had an open head wound, and we both had concussions. My arms were frozen as if they were still gripping the steering wheel. It was pretty scary. We could have died in that accident.

The day after the accident, I took Amira to her family doctor to get checked out. She said to her doctor, "My husband and I were involved in a serious rollover accident on 1-75 last night." Her doctor responded, "Oh my God! Was that you in the white SUV? I saw it on the news. That SUV looked as if no one could have survived the accident. I am so glad you are here!"

A couple of days later, I was looking for a new vehicle. I felt we would be safer if we drove a larger vehicle, like a Lincoln Navigator. I was watching the local news that evening when I heard that a Lincoln Navigator had flipped over on the same expressway we rolled over on. The people in that car died.

Amira's account of the accident

I remember very little of the accident because I was unconscious after the first rollover. When we returned home, I said to Omar, "God has a purpose for us to live. We are still here."

Despite this huge speed bump on my journey, I kept crawling on my highway. I had come too far for it to end here. I didn't waiver in my commitment to present at a convention the following week. I wore makeup to cover my bumps and bruises and did not let the accident stand in my way. This accident was a huge obstacle in my highway to success. To this day, the ringing in my ears continues. We thank God every day for being alive. You never know what tomorrow will bring. I believe that God has a plan for us. This chapter in our life was not the end of a journey, as it could have been, but an opportunity to push forward with a new appreciation for life and each other.

Chapter 18

Acupuncture and Reiki

I always felt that I was supposed to help other people. My friend, Ester, lived in Farmington and worked as an acupressure practitioner. She invited me to one of her circle sessions to see what she does with ear acupressure and beads. She didn't make much money, but she liked helping people feel better. I found it to be very interesting.

We met again at a senior fair at the Costic Activities Center in Farmington, MI, where I had rented a table to demonstrate activities for people with dementia and hopefully sell some of my books and activities. People were standing in line for Ester's acupressure treatments. They were saying how much better they felt after the treatment. Some said it gave them more energy, less anxiety, and more positive thoughts. She gave acupressure treatments to 40 or 50 people, and everyone said they felt better.

I was impressed with the results she achieved with just her fingers and small beads placed in the ear. Esther said for a fee of $450, she would teach me how to use acupressure and magnetic beads. It was something that made a difference in people's lives, and I felt like I wanted to do this for caregivers. Caregivers help as much as they can when it comes to Alzheimer's, but they don't get much support for their well-being. I wanted to learn more, so I paid her, and she taught me her techniques.

I found a course that taught auricular acupuncture at The Lincoln Recovery Center Hospital in Bronx, NY, taught by the founder of the National Acupuncture Detoxification Association (NADA), Dr. Michael Smith. NADA is an organization dedicated to helping drug addicts overcome withdrawal from drug abuse, with non-drug treatment. The treatment was so effective that it became a mandatory treatment in the New York court system for recovering addicts. I could become NADA certified to perform acupuncture and acupressure if I completed the 80-hour course successfully. In 2010, I registered for the course, and Omar drove me to Bronx, New York, to train under Dr. Smith.

Omar arranged for me to stay with a woman named Kathy who worked at the hospital. It was for a couple of weeks for $50 a night. Staying with her meant that I always had a ride to class and a ride back to her apartment. Driving around New York for me would have been suicide and a taxi would be scary.

I stayed on the sixth floor of an old apartment building in one of her spare bedrooms. The other spare bedroom was rented the next day to a male student. Omar stayed the first night to make me feel better. The elevator creaked and rumbled like it was falling apart. It shook like a 7.0 earthquake. Climbing up the dim-lit back stairway was even scarier. As we got ready for bed, I saw cockroaches running around and mouse tracks on the floor, and it freaked me out.

I told Omar, "I want to go back with you in the morning. I can't stay here! I don't know if I can take this for two weeks. I don't want to be here!"

"Amira, why? You are here already!" Omar said.

"I don't like this place. I don't know what to do. I feel like this arrangement isn't going to work out." Eventually, Omar convinced me the sacrifices I was making would be worth it. If I stuck it out, I would be certified to use needles in my acupuncture treatment. In Michigan, the NADA protocol certification would qualify me as an acupuncturist.

The next day, the guy that rented the other room arrived. He came from California to train as an auricular acupuncturist. One bedroom was for him, and the other bedroom was for me.

On the first night alone, I studied by myself until 2:00 a.m. As soon as I laid down to get some sleep, I felt the bed move and shake. At first, I thought it might be a cat or another animal. I moved to the other side of the bed, and it started to shake even more. I jumped out of bed terrified and ran to Kathy's room. "Oh my God! Kathy! Kathy!" I screamed.

She was sleeping and snoring loudly. I couldn't awaken her. I asked myself, "What am I going to do now?" I went back to my room and left the light on for the rest of the night so I could see what was going on in my room, but I couldn't sleep.

In the morning, Kathy knocked on the door and said, "Amira, it's time to wake up."

I was already awake and dizzy because I was sitting there all night and had not closed my eyes. I opened the door, and she greeted me with a smile and, "Good morning! Did you sleep well?"

"Kathy, I want to speak with you! What is going on here? My bed was shaking all night!"

"Really?" she said. Then she smiled.

"Why are you smiling? What's going on??" I asked.

"That was my husband."

"What do you mean, your husband?" I asked.

"My husband died five years ago, and his spirit is here."

"You mean a ghost?" I asked.

"Yes, but don't worry about it. My husband's ghost won't hurt you," Kathy said.

"Oh my God! Now where am I going to go?"

I needed to rest so I could study because if I didn't do well, I would not get certified. I was upset and swearing. "Amira, Amira! You're going to be okay," she said. Kathy was used to everything. She was a tough lady.

When the guy in the other room woke up, I asked him if he felt something last night. "Like what?" he asked. I replied, "I don't know. I guess I'm just curious." I didn't tell him about my night because I wanted to hear from him first. The next day, he said he felt strange things while he was in bed. I told him I did too.

While Kathy was driving me to Lincoln Hospital, she said, "You know what? You can sleep in the bed with me." I told her I preferred she slept in my room. The bed in my room was larger than hers, and maybe I could move away from her constant snoring.

When I arrived at the Lincoln Recovery Center, I spoke to my instructor, Rosa. I told her I was not doing well, and I was in deep trouble being here. I told her about not being able to sleep all night because my bed was moving by itself, and I was afraid. I told her I didn't think I could continue to lose sleep and concentrate in class.

"Kathy didn't tell you about the room before you rented it?" Rosa asked.

"No one told me anything like this would happen. Have you heard about strange things happening at Kathy's house?" I asked.

"No, but if there is anything strange about that room, Kathy should have told you about it. You can stop this by putting some salt in a cup of water and setting it under your bed. This should keep any spirits from bothering you."

That night, when it was time for bed, I told Kathy, "You're going to sleep in my bed, or I'm calling my husband to come and pick me up."

So we slept together in my room. I slept with my head at the top of the bed, and Kathy slept with her head at the bottom. As I began to fall asleep, the bed started to go BOOM, BOOM, BOOM again! Kathy was still snoring. I had put salt under my bed, but it didn't seem to work.

"Kathy?" I hollered. I thought I was going crazy. "Kathy?" I screamed again.

She finally awoke and asked, "What?!"

"The bed is jumping again!"

"Go to bed!" Kathy told me.

I couldn't sleep. I turned the light on and sat there all night studying. I didn't know what else to do. Was it a ghost? I called Omar in the morning and asked him to pick me up, but he said, "Amira, I'm not going to pick you up. You have a goal. You have to be strong." He thought that if I could get through these two weeks, in these living conditions, it would strengthen my will to succeed.

Night after night, I kept the light on. But after a while, I became annoyed with my living conditions. I told Kathy, "You know what? I don't want you to sleep in my room anymore."

"What do you mean, you don't want me to sleep here? I'll be good," she said. "Are you sure? What are you going to do now?"

"Yes, I want you to go back to your room. I want to be by myself, and I want to take care of this ghost," I said.

I sat in my bed all night by myself with the light on. If a ghost or a spirit came, I wanted to see it and confront my fear, face-to-face. I was determined to take care of the ghost problem myself. I felt like I could handle this on my own. My anger at this ghost had become stronger than my fear. I left the light on every night. For the rest of my stay, I felt something was around, but it didn't bother me. The bed never rumbled and shook again. Finally, I could get some sleep.

We were eating breakfast one morning when Kathy asked her granddaughter, who was visiting, to get something from my room. She said, "No, I don't want to go in that room. You know I don't go in there by myself. It's scary." Kathy went to the room herself. I thought, "Everyone already knew about this room except me. Am I the only one who didn't know?"

Kathy was driving us to the hospital one morning when she told me that someone had been shot in this area. We had not gone this way before. I asked, "Why are we heading this way?" It was dark and looked scary.

"This is the route we have to go so I can drop off a package to a patient. We have to do this," she answered.

"I'm so scared," I said.

"Amira, don't worry about it...if you die, you die," Kathy replied. She wasn't worried.

It was clearly a dangerous area. We had to drop off a package from the hospital to someone at an apartment building, and I was scared the whole time. The hallways were dimly-lit, and the smell of cannabis was thick in the air. I'm sure there was drug activity in the building. I don't know how we made it out of there alive. I prayed the entire time we were in that building. Maybe that helped keep us safe.

Kathy grew up on the streets. She was a former alcoholic and drug addict. One day, I asked her, "Tell me about your life when you were in your 20s."

She replied, "I don't know. I don't remember anything from back then. My memory burned out from heavy alcohol use. I was stoned all the time."

I said, "Really?"

She said, "Yes, I can't remember anything. It seemed like everyone I hung around with had some type of addiction." That was what Lincoln Recovery Center Hospital was all about. In the Bronx, New York, anyone convicted of drug abuse had to, by law, get treatment at the Lincoln Recovery Center. Many people came in for drug rehab every day.

There was no better place for students to learn than from real people with real problems. We learned the techniques in the class and trained on each other before treating drug addicts. After we learned the techniques, we practiced on real drug addicts who were coming in by court order to fulfill their mandated obligation. In addition to the actual treatment of real severe addictions, we had the best mentor, Dr. Michael Smith, who was amazing. He guided us and supervised our skills. Where else can you get that type of experience and education but from the founder of the organization? People came from all over the world to train and learn Dr. Smith's acupuncture protocol. I was training with the best.

We inserted needles in the particular five points in the ear. The sympathetic point has a calming effect, and others were the shen men, the lung, liver, and kidney. Each of the five points played a role in recovery and detoxification from drugs. It helped people cope with coming down from alcohol, smoking, eating disorders, or almost any addiction. When students practiced on me, I felt calm and relaxed. I loved it. When toxins are removed from their system, some people feel euphoric emotions. I was amazed to hear testimony from so many addicts.

Two days before completing the course, the instructor introduced us to Reiki, a relaxation treatment. I had never heard of Reiki, and couldn't even pronounce it right. I wasn't the only one. Everyone had questions, "What is Reiki? What is it for?" We learned that the Japanese word is derived from two words. Rei means "God's wisdom" or "The higher power," and Ki means "Life force energy." It was brought here from Japan in the late 1920s.

We went into a large room and sat in a large circle. Two trainers entered the room and one said, "You will feel the energy around you. Maybe you will see colors, and maybe you won't. Each of you may feel the energy in different ways. You will feel natural energy healing your body." I had no clue what she was talking about, but I followed whatever we were instructed to do. I was there to learn. The teachers were on each side of the circle. It took about two hours for everyone to get a treatment, because feeling the energy took longer on some people than others. The instructors put their hands above each student's head until they could feel the energy and see an aura appear. It took about 3 to 5 minutes for each person. As the instructors moved around the room, they asked each person to close their eyes, relax, and feel the energy.

I was exhausted, but I tried to relax while others were receiving Reiki treatment. Almost immediately after closing my eyes, I saw a vision of a beautiful woman. The image was right in front of my face. She was a beautiful woman who, in my mind, resembled Mother Mary. Her eyes were a beautiful blue color, contrasted by her white skin, rosy cheeks, and red lips. She wore a flowing white dress. Above the blue scarf that adorned her head, and covered her shoulders, was a glowing purple ring. I felt close to her in spirit. She had a beautiful, calming smile. A voice whispered to me, "This is Mother Mary." All I could think of is, "Oh my God! Is this real?"

I loved it so much. I was at peace, and I did not want to open my eyes. I kept my eyes closed. Mother Mary smiled as she started to rise into the air like she was floating. Then I began to float up with her. She smiled at me again, and I went higher with her. I saw myself with her, and every time she floated higher, I floated with her. I said, "Oh my God, I feel so high. I don't want to leave earth. I want to go back to earth." I kept wishing I could go back to earth. We began descending, and I followed her back to earth. She then ascended again into the sky, but this time she didn't take me with her. Slowly, I opened my eyes. It wasn't my turn yet for my Reiki treatment, so I closed my eyes again. I was feeling the energy and seeing purple and white colors when I closed my eyes.

Whenever I closed my eyes, Mother Mary was already there for me. She never left. She was still there, smiling at me, even after the hour-long session of Reiki. My recollection of this occurrence was so vivid that I still remember it, in detail, to this day.

Now it was my turn. I had already felt the energy in the room. The Reiki session was unusual, because when the instructor asked me to close my eyes, the visions of Mother Mary continued. I was completely peaceful and relaxed.

After the Reiki session, a lady came to me and asked, "Amira, would you like to learn how to give Reiki treatments?" She was a Reiki teacher.

"Why do you ask?" I said.

"I feel like you can heal people," she said.

"Heal people?" I asked in a surprised voice.

"Yes, what's the matter?" she asked.

I said, "I saw something you won't believe."

"Oh, I will believe you!" she reassured me.

I confided to her, "I saw a vision of Mother Mary."

She gasped and said, "What! You saw Mother Mary? I have been trying very hard to see her for years, and she came to you?"

"Yes, I'm telling you the truth!" I said. She promised not to tell anyone.

"I see why you didn't tell anyone. You are a lucky person. You have a gift. Oh my God, tell me about it, honey. It's very rare for Mother Mary to come to anyone."

I told her that every time I saw Mother Mary, I would always be floating high up with her, and I would become scared and ask to come down. She laughed and said, "Oh my God, tell me more, tell me more!" I told her about seeing Jesus, and she said, "I believe you." She was not surprised. "I felt something different about you," she said.

A moment passed, and she said, "You know what, I normally charge $250. I'll only charge you $100 to train. I really want to help you. You are an extraordinary person."

She continued, "I can tell you with certainty, you are a healer. I saw it, and I felt it. You know what? It's not fair if you don't do Reiki when you're able to heal people. I can't believe no one ever told you about your gift."

"Yes, more than one person told me," I said.

"When did you hear this? Who told you?" she asked.

I shared with her, "When I was about 12 years old, in Lebanon, a psychic told me I had a gift to heal people. As an adult, I was told by an American Indian psychic that I was a healer."

I continued, "I saw a famous healer on the Doctor Oz show. My husband and I attended a conference where he was healing people. I talked with him after the conference and told him about myself. He told me I was a natural healer, but I didn't take him seriously. I thought he might say this to everyone."

She replied, "He was right. Even when you are talking to people, you heal them. You are an amazing lady."

I completed the acupuncture course at the Lincoln Recovery Center and received my NADA acupuncture certification, Auricular Acupuncture Detox Specialist. I was hopeful that auricular acupuncture would help relieve the symptoms of Alzheimer's and also relieve stress for the caregivers.

After seeing the power of Reiki, I decided to take a Reiki course with a Reiki master teacher in Ohio. It was a 3-hour drive from home, but she was the best Reiki Master I could find, with many years of experience. The first class was one of three levels. After completing the third level, I passed and became a Reiki Master and Teacher. The Reiki master told me I had a very powerful healing spirit.

Initially, Omar wasn't too excited about my Reiki treatments. Some people believed in Reiki, and some didn't. I wanted to try Reiki on Omar, but he did not agree right away. For two years, I asked him to let me give him a Reiki treatment. He was an engineer, and he told me he did not believe in hocus-pocus. "But if it helps others, God will bless you for doing it," he said.

But when Omar started to see how much better people felt after my treatment, he began to reconsider that possibly it was real. Omar was going through some stressful situations and wasn't sleeping well. For two months, he was only getting two or three hours of sleep a night. I begged him, "Let me give you a Reiki treatment."

He finally agreed. For the first time in months, he had a full night's rest, sleeping for eight hours. He agreed it might have been the Reiki. On another occasion, Omar had stomach pains while we were relaxing on the couch watching TV. He said the pain was getting worse instead of better, so I asked, "Maybe if I give you a Reiki and acupuncture treatment, you will feel better." He replied, "You know I don't believe in hocus-pocus, but okay, let's do it. It's worth a try." He remembered that it worked when he had a sleeping problem.

During the Reiki treatment, I felt exactly where his pain was. When I pointed to where it was hurting, Omar said it was the right spot. "Can you feel the heat?" I asked.

"No, I can't feel the heat," he replied.

Then I touched his body, and he said it felt like a hot iron. He felt the heat through his shirt, as if it was going to burn him. The pain in his stomach began to subside. Even though he didn't believe in Reiki, he conceded that it works. He didn't say he was a believer, but he was more receptive to at least allow me to try it on him. He needed proof that anything is real. The fact is, when he was not sleeping well, he slept through the night after my treatment. His stomach pains went away after my treatment. Both times my treatment worked for Omar.

Sometimes, as I am giving a Reiki treatment, I see Jesus. Something tells me it is Jesus. When I close my eyes, the vision of him appears. He is a beautiful man with long, curly hair, olive colored skin, and green-blue eyes. I only see him from the neck up. When I would see his gentle smile, I knew it must be Jesus. I was not scared at all. I still focused on performing Reiki. Sometimes I mention to the person I am giving a Reiki treatment the vision I saw above them. Sometimes the vision I describe is a loved one who has passed. The vision usually stayed for 5 to 10 seconds. It would come and go, but always exuded comfort and peace.

Many top hospitals provide Reiki treatments to complement their traditional protocol. Henry Ford Hospital offers Reiki to assist with the healing process in their facilities. I have had doctors, dentists, and other professionals ask me for Reiki treatments. Others have told me I am a healer, and insist I am gifted with this power.

One day, a priest called me, and he sounded desperate. His voice was quivering. He asked, "I heard about you and your Reiki treatments. Do you have time tomorrow to give me a Reiki and acupuncture treatment?"

"Yes," I said.

"How much do you charge?" he asked.

"It doesn't matter. I won't charge you," I told the priest.

He made an appointment with me. I fit him in my schedule because he sounded desperate for help. When the treatment ended, he opened his eyes and stared straight into my eyes. I asked him if he was okay and he said, "Yes, I'm alright. Now I know what Reiki is all about. It is about you. You are amazing." He hugged me and said, "I'm delighted that I came. I feel much better now."

If I see something bad happen to someone, I usually pray for them. I pray for the victim to live and get back to good health. When I pray, I pray from the bottom of my heart. When I feel a chill, I know my prayers are answered. In addition, I know my prayers are answered when I get goose bumps.

I asked a lady from church named Roberta, "I don't know why I am getting these feelings." She replied, "Oh, it might be because God is answering your prayers."

Each time I get chills or goose bumps when I pray, I say to myself, "I hope God is hearing my prayers and healing people." I don't know the answer, but I will continue to pray whenever I see a need. No one has all of the answers. I believe that everyone would like to think that someone is praying for them.

Chapter 19
My Visions

A few years ago, something amazing happened. Omar typically came home late from work, so I called him to check on him. "Omar, when are you coming home?"

"Amira, I won't be coming home anytime soon. I need to finish my project," he said.

It was around 11:00 pm. My bed was near a window I was facing. I looked out the window and saw a purple flash of light, then a rainbow. It disappeared after a few seconds.

"Was that Mother Mary??" I asked myself.

When I thought it possibly could be Mother Mary, she appeared and smiled. She was clasping a white scarf in her folded hands. Her eyes were blue, and she had rosy lips. There was a colorful aura, like a shimmering rainbow, over her head. It was glowing like a light.

I wasn't scared at all. "Oh my God, is this Mother Mary?!" I asked myself.

It was a beautiful and peaceful feeling. We looked at each other eye to eye, and then I turned over in bed to follow a small white dove that appeared to fly over my head.

"Oh my God, it's a dove!" I exclaimed.

It was flying near the ceiling, and I kept following it toward the bedroom door. The dove flew around the door for a few moments then disappeared through the doorway. I turned back toward the window, and Mother Mary was gone. "If I tell Omar, he will think I'm going crazy. I will tell him later, not tonight." No one would believe me! Days later, I told Omar, and he was amazed with what I shared with him. I said the experience felt like the most intense love and peace.

Omar took me to an antique store in Ohio. As I was shopping, I came upon a statue of Mother Mary. It looked exactly like the vision I had of her! The scarf and her smile were unmistakable.

"Oh, my God!" I exclaimed.

"What?" Omar said.

"Look! Look!" I exclaimed again.

Mother Mary was looking at me the same way she had in my vision. "Omar! This statue is an exact image of what I saw in my vision!"

He wanted to buy it for me, but I said it was too much money. He told me it was unusual, and I might regret not buying it. I told me I would buy it another time. Buying the statue wasn't on my mind because we were busy with other things.

I thought about it every day for a week, and finally said to Omar, "I keep thinking about the statue of Mother Mary. I want to go back and buy it." We went back to the same store, but it was gone. I said, "Omar, let's go to another antique store. Maybe we will find the same statue of Mother Mary there." We went to dozens of places over the next year. We went back to that same store half a dozen times, hoping maybe they moved it or we missed it. Each time I returned to the store, I said to myself, "Mother Mary, please come back. I promise I will get you. I will buy you this time." Unfortunately this never happened.

I started sharing more visions with Omar. Everywhere I went, I saw visions. I didn't have to go to bed. I just closed my eyes and saw people close to my face. I saw my sister come to me, crying for help. I had strangers coming to me for help. It was so amazing.

My cousin, Siham, lived in Canada. Her son, Samer, 21 years old, was studying in Australia to become a pharmacist. He went with his friend to spend some time near the ocean. While he and his friend were sitting on a large rock, a huge wave hit them from behind and swept them into the water. His friend was seriously injured but survived. My cousin's son was missing. Authorities called Siham and informed her about the tragedy and asked if she could come to Australia to help with the search and identify his body.

Miada, another relative, called and told me Samer was missing. I had never met Samer, and didn't know what he looked like. I closed my eyes, and I saw him. He was curled up under a rock in clear, blue water. He was skinny, had dark-colored skin, and short black hair. I asked myself, "Is this him?"

The next morning, I called Miada. "I want to tell you something, but you promise you won't tell anyone?"

"I won't tell anyone, I swear!"

"Is he short and skinny with black hair?"

"Yes! You never met him?"

"I have never met him or seen a picture of him," I said.

"Then how do you know what he looks like?"

"I saw him in my vision. But I am afraid he may be dead. I saw him pinned under a rock, curled up on his side." I told her exactly what I saw in my vision.

"Oh my God! You think he didn't make it?"

"It looks like it, but hopefully I am wrong."

A week later, they found his body in the water, partially covered by a rock in a fetal position. My vision was real.

A few months later, Omar and I watched a Dr. Oz show about a healer named Dr. Issam Nemeh. Coincidentally, an advertisement piece arrived in the mail soon thereafter announcing that Dr. Nemeh was coming to Livonia, MI, for six weeks. It cost $200 for each person, though. I said to Omar, "I want to go. Do you want to go?" He wasn't excited about it, but he said yes to please me.

Dr. Nemeh stayed in Livonia for six weeks. Many, many people came to his daily sessions to witness the healing or to be healed. He was clearly a celebrity. I was fascinated with his skills, so we went to see him in person.

Omar and I sat in the tenth row, which was pretty far from the podium. When Dr. Nemeh spoke, everyone was so quiet, you could hear a pin drop. There was a large picture of Jesus behind him. In front of me was a taller guy. I had to move my head to the left to see Dr. Nemeh. As I was looking, I had a feeling this guy in front of me was not healthy.

"Omar! The guy in front of us is sick." Omar replied, "How do you know he's sick?" I said, "I don't know. I just know he is very sick."

I had seen a sign in the aura that showed the guy in front of me was not well. I can see auras. A short time later, the same guy got up to go to the bathroom. He was walking strangely, and I said, "Omar! I told you!"

"You're right, he is sick. I thought it was his wife who was sick because of how she looked."

When Dr. Nemeh finished the lecture, anyone who wished to get healed walked to the front of the room and stood in line. He went up to each person, held their hand, and most would fall backward while his assistant caught them. What happened next was amazing. While Dr. Nemeh was praying and holding his hand on each person's head, I witnessed both he and the picture of Jesus had beautiful yellow auras around their heads.

"Wow, I can't believe it," I whispered to myself.

Some of the people he was praying for had an aura, and some did not. I believe some people were blessed, and some were not. Dr. Nemeh and the picture of Jesus had the same aura at the same time. I asked Omar, "Do you see what I see?"

"What? Where?" he asked.

"Look above Dr. Nemeh's head. Do you see anything?" I asked.

"I am looking, and I see Dr. Nemeh. What you are talking about?" Omar asked.

"Okay, I just wanted to make sure you don't see the same thing I do," I said.

Dr. Nemeh prayed for every person who came to him, and the aura remained around his head the entire time. I said, "Omar, the person Dr. Nemeh is praying for now won't be healed."

Omar asked, "How do you know that?"

"Because I don't see an aura," I replied.

Omar was beginning to get irritated with me. He was trying to focus on the event, while I was predicting who would get healed and who would not. "I guess I can see it, and you can't," I said.

I continued to whisper in Omar's ear, "She's healed, he's not healed." I was having fun predicting who I thought got healed and who did not by looking for their aura.

During the bathroom break, I saw Dr. Nemeh's wife standing near the doorway, surrounded by a group of people, all asking questions. The crowd moved to Dr. Nemeh when he came through the door. I went up to her while everyone was around the doctor. I looked into his wife's eyes, and she looked at me as if she was ready to hear something from me.

I said to her, "I have a question."

"What is it?" she replied.

"That is a picture of Jesus, right?"

"Yes, it is Jesus," she responded.

I told her, "I can see an aura surrounding the picture of Jesus. I was sitting far from the small picture and couldn't tell if it was Jesus until I saw the aura. I also saw an aura around your husband." She was very surprised by what I was saying and said, "Really? Oh my God! Not many people can see auras. Can I talk to you after the program? You are a fascinating person!"

Everyone returned to their seats after the break. An assistant went row to row and asked who else would like to get healed. When it was my turn, I walked up to the podium. Dr. Nemeh placed his hand on my forehead and prayed for me, and when he gave me a nudge rearward, his assistant gently guided me to lay down. I kept my eyes closed for a few moments and focused on what just took place.

I continued to images of the people with auras and without auras. I learned so much about myself at this healing conference.

When the session was over, Dr. Nemeh's wife came to me. "Can you do me a favor?" she asked. "Can you write down your name and your phone number?"

I said, "Okay." She appeared to believe everything I shared with her.

We exchanged business cards. She then asked, "Can I contact you sometime soon?"

I said, "Of course! I would be happy to talk with you."

Later, she sent an email and said, "I want to share your gift with the rest of the world. Maybe someone like Dr. Oz might be interested in your amazing gift, or perhaps a news channel would like to interview you. Please send me your story and I will forward it to an associate at Harvard. He was on the Dr. Oz Show with Dr. Nemeh."

I wrote down everything I had seen at Dr. Nemeh's healing session and sent the information to Channel 7 news in Detroit, MI. I didn't hear back from the news editor or Dr. Oz, but I felt good about getting validation of my gift from a well-known healer.

After attending Dr. Nemeh's healing session, I became more confident in my ability to have visions and recognize auras. Some auras are as colorful as a rainbow, while others are pure white. Often I see auras on people attending my workshops. Many visions also come to me while giving Reiki sessions. One woman I was giving a Reiki session to was severely depressed. During the session, I saw a man's figure above her body, from the chest up, wearing a military hat. He had blonde hair and a handsome face. He thanked me for helping her. I knew he must be someone she knows.

After the session, I asked if she knew a man resembling my vision. "Oh my God, yes!" she said. She started crying hysterically, and as she was sobbing said, "Yes, it was him! He passed away a month ago from a heart attack."

"Well, I want you to be happy knowing he's here with you, and he knows I am taking care of you," I said.

"Oh my God! Did he tell you anything?"

"No, he didn't give me any message for you. He just looked at me and thanked me. That's all," I said.

She sobbed, "Oh my God! I feel better now."

When I focus on a person and wish the best for them, they feel it from me. I feel like a hero because it comes from inside me. I felt it when I was a little girl, and now I can help others feel better by sharing this gift from God. I believe if you wish people well, wellness will come back to you.

Omar never encouraged me to talk about my visions. It wasn't that he didn't believe me, but he didn't think I should talk about them. Omar understood my special gift, and that God intended it for me. He often asked if I was a psychic, and I would reply, "I am only telling you what I see."

Omar's niece, Pamela, lived in New York, ate healthy foods, exercised, was a yoga teacher and avid bicyclist, and ran the Boston Marathon many times. She worked as a librarian. Her life was relatively stress-free.

I was in the kitchen at our home and I was talking to Omar, thinking he was near me. He wasn't responding, so I called out to him. He answered and said he was upstairs in the bathroom.

As I turned, I saw someone come from our bedroom to the family room. I knew it wasn't Omar. He was upstairs in the bathroom. It was a shadow figure, possibly Omar's Mom. I went to the stairway and called Omar again.

"I'm upstairs in the bathroom," he replied again.

"Oh my God!" I said. It wasn't him. I went back to the kitchen, and this time I saw Omar's Mom walking through the kitchen.

All I could think of is something terrible was going to happen. Three days later, in late December 2009, Pamela died of a heart attack. She was just 50 years old. It shocked everyone because she appeared to be healthy.

About four years after Pamela died, I saw Omar's Dad come the same way that his Mom came, from our bedroom, down the steps, and to the family room, where we have a fireplace. I had never seen his Dad before, or even a picture of him.

I asked Omar, "Was your father fairly short and thin with very little hair on the sides?"

"Yes, that sounds like my dad," he said.

"I think I saw him."

Omar's brother, Joe, was very sick. I didn't think he was going to die, but I had a bad feeling about this vision. I prayed this dark shadow vision wasn't going to mean the same thing as the one about Omar's Mom. I did not have a good feeling. I didn't tell Omar about my warning. Omar's brother died two months after I saw the vision of Omar's Dad.

One time, Omar and I were in Las Vegas playing penny slot machines. Suddenly I saw a vision of flames surrounding me. I thought, "I hope this doesn't mean something bad is about to happen again." The visions continued appearing after we returned home. I kept asking myself, "What's going on? Why do I see flames? I hope nothing terrible happens."

A few days after arriving home, I heard that my nephew, Ben, had a severe car accident. His car went under a semi-trailer and wedged under the truck. He was facing death, but he made it. It was a miracle he didn't die. I said to myself, "That must have been the bad omen of seeing the flames."

Omar's Faith and Spirit in the Hospital

In November 2014, my best friend, soul mate, and husband, Omar, had routine surgery early in the day to correct a deviated septum. I was not too concerned because it was an outpatient procedure. Everything went fine, so we were relaxing at home watching the television, as we usually do at the end of the day. The only thing different was that Omar had a bandage covering the front of his nose. Later in the evening, he said he felt tightness in his chest. It started to worry me because two years ago, he had similar but much worse symptoms, including pain that resulted in needing a heart stent. I had cause to worry.

The tightness seemed to go away, so we went to bed, but only for a few hours. Around 3 am, Omar awoke with increased chest tightness. I insisted we call 911. Henry Ford Hospital was the closest hospital with an ER. Doctors were concerned it was another blocked artery. He was given blood thinners to prevent a blood clot. It caused his nose to bleed continuously. He had a heart catheterization that indicated a blocked artery was likely the cause of his symptoms. The doctor said Omar needed stents again. Stent procedures were not available at this hospital. With all of the tubes and IV connected, they transferred Omar to Beaumont Hospital, where two years ago, his cardiologist implanted stents. It was Friday morning, and Omar would have to wait until Monday before the surgeon could place the stents in his blocked arteries.

Omar is semi-claustrophobic and was not feeling comfortable. I never left his side. By Saturday evening, Omar was very uncomfortable, and he was panicking. The medication he was taking every eight hours to calm him down was no longer working. He was panicked and couldn't stand it anymore. He asked for more medication, but the nurse said it was too soon. It had been only four hours since he took the last pill. He was sitting on the edge of the hospital bed in sheer terror. I asked if he wanted me to give him a Reiki treatment. He said no, nothing would help. Omar continued to shake and sweat in terror. The blood thinner he needed for his heart was causing his nose to bleed profusely. He couldn't breathe and blood was running down the back of his throat. He thought he might not make it.

After a few moments, he changed his mind and said he was willing to try anything. He begged me to hurry. He said he would lie down for two minutes for me to do Reiki, because he was not sure he could lay down longer than that. He slept for maybe ten minutes as I gave him the Reiki treatment, and when he woke up, he sat up completely relaxed, and his panic and anxiety were gone. He was in disbelief. Omar was blown away by the Reiki. He turned from a skeptic into a believer. It brought him peace in a very stressful situation without the use of drugs. He was amazed!

He said he wished I had given him the treatment later in the evening, so he would be able to sleep. I reassured him, "Don't worry. It will last a few days." Thankfully, he slept through each night that he stayed in the hospital.

I was worried about Omar's procedure. I prayed as they wheeled Omar into the prep room on Monday morning to prepare him for the heart catheterization. I prayed until I got tired of praying and rested my mind. When he went in for the procedure, the attendant ushered me to a waiting room. Something told me to continue praying feverishly for him, that he needed my prayers. I closed my eyes and began praying as I've never prayed before. I began praying ten minutes after they wheeled him into the operating room. I felt myself rise to the top of the room, just floating up. Looking down, all I could see was Omar's body lying on a narrow table, and he seemed to be in pain. His face was straining. He had told me that when he had a similar procedure two years ago, there wasn't any pain. So why did he look like he was in pain? I didn't see any doctors or nurses. He didn't look like a vision. It was him. I was concerned that he was alone. I prayed even harder for him. While I was still praying, I heard a nurse call my name. "Mrs. Tame! Mrs. Tame!" I could feel myself come from a higher place back down to myself.

"They found blocked arteries in your husband's heart, and placed stents to correct the blockage. He is doing fine."

Omar's Account of His Experience

Amira provided all the support I needed during this episode in my life. I didn't want other family members by my side. It seems like I am reminded of how sick I am when I see many concerned faces surrounding me, and this might be serious. I just wanted to get it over with, get back home, and enjoy the week vacation that I scheduled before getting sick. I was not happy to hear that I needed another procedure, but I was not terrified because I had been there before. I didn't expect to experience any discomfort. Boy, was I wrong!

About ten minutes into the procedure, I began to feel pain in my heart. Trying hard not to be a crybaby, I didn't say anything initially to the doctor. I said to myself, "I'll just tough it out." It got worse, and I thought if Amira were here and saw me wincing and tightening my lip, she would ask me if I felt okay. She would ask the doctor, "What's wrong with my husband? Do something for him!" The pain got to the point that I finally blurted, "Doc, is it supposed to hurt this much? It hurts really bad!" I heard the doctor say, "Give him more Nitro!"

The pain was reduced but still there. A few moments later, the pain got really bad again. I told the doctor it was still hurting badly, and he again ordered an increase in Nitro. All I could think of is "I wish Amira were here." If she saw me wincing in pain, she would have alerted the doctor right away. What if something went wrong and I didn't see her again? I wanted her to know I was hurting. I knew she was on the next floor, in the surgery waiting room, and had no clue as to what I was going through.

Suddenly, I felt peaceful and without pain. The doctor said, "Okay, Omar, we are finished. All we have to do is remove the tubes. You did fine." Thankfully it was over.

When Amira came into the recovery room, she asked me worriedly, "Are you okay?"

"Yes, everything went fine," I said. I didn't want to worry Amira with the painful details.

"Are you sure?" she said. "Did you feel any pain?"

"Well, yes, some pain. It was more painful than the first time." Amira then told me about her experience seeing me from above, in pain, while she was praying. The timing was right on. I knew she actually saw me as I was thinking about her and wanting her to be with me. I believe that without her prayers, I might not be here writing this.

Now back to me. I believe that when I pray from the bottom of my heart, my prayers are heard. The story about Omar's experience at the hospital is testimony that prayers are heard. I pray for everyone, even for strangers. When I'm driving, and I see an accident, no matter where I'm going, I will stop and pray for those involved in the accident.

I always prayed for my friend Mary Shoucair when I felt she needed a prayer. She didn't believe in traditional medicine or traditional doctors. She believed healthy eating, exercise, and prayer would keep her well.

One day, while I was driving Mary to the grocery store, she showed me her irritated finger. I asked her what happened. She said it was nothing. It happened after she handled fertilizer while feeding her plants. To me, it didn't look good at all. I recommended she see a doctor. She thought this idea was absurd since it was only a scratch, and there was no way she would see a doctor for such a ridiculous reason. I could see it was swollen and had a rash. I insisted we go straight to the ER, and I was firm with her. I said, "I know you don't like doctors, but make an exception for me just this time." When I promised to buy her lunch afterward, she finally agreed.

I waited for two hours while a doctor diagnosed her swollen finger. Finally, I was allowed to see her. There was an IV in her arm and a bag of fluid dripping medication. She said the doctor diagnosed her with acute blood poisoning from the chemicals in the fertilizer, and they wanted to keep her to cleanse her blood. The doctor told her if she had not received medical attention right away, it could have been fatal. For two months, I drove her to the clinic for treatment until her blood was clean. Mary told everyone I saved her life.

After she recovered from this episode, whenever Mary felt pain, or she was not feeling well, she would call and ask me to pray for her. Mary was a highly educated person, and I learned much about life from her. She saw something special in me. She trusted me with all of her good and bad stories. My intuition and determination may have saved Mary's life. Why was I so insistent that Mary see a doctor right away? Maybe it was a voice from an angel saying, "Your friend is in trouble."

On another occasion, I was again in the right place at the right time. I took Mary to the hospital with a protruding hernia in her abdomen. I waited in her hospital room until the procedure was complete and she returned to her room. She was still coming out of sedation. To me, she didn't look well. She was pale and very weak. I called the nurse to check on Mary to see what was wrong. The nurse seemed irritated and said, "Miss, she just came out of surgery. This is normal. She is okay." I said, "No, she is not okay. I want to talk to the surgeon." She told me he was in surgery with another patient. I said, "I don't care. I want to see a doctor right now." The surgeon came and took one look at her and wheeled her back to surgery. They discovered she had internal bleeding and needed emergency surgery to correct it. When she came back to her room the second time, she looked and felt much better.

What caused me to challenge the hospital staff, the nurse, and the doctor? Why did I not accept the answers I was getting? I didn't give up.

I kept fighting because something told me to do so! Maybe it was a spirit or guardian angel.

Mary had not forgotten this until she passed away at 96 years old. I still pray for her to be at peace. God rest her soul. I miss her.

Fear Never Left Me

Fear is something I will probably always live with. It has stayed with me wherever I am. A fear of not understanding something, a fear of being wrong about something, a fear of going the wrong way always obstructs the view of the road ahead of me. My life was riddled with anxiety. If fear of my abusive Dad or abusive teachers wasn't enough, there is more.

My fear of lightning wasn't from my Dad's treatment, but from an unusual experience in Lebanon. Mom and Dad had gone shopping. Nada and I were playing in our bedroom during a big storm, with booming sounds of lightening. There was a small window near the ceiling that was open. I was afraid to stay in that room during the storm, so I grabbed Nada's hand and led her into the living room.

As we entered the living room, I looked back and saw a blinding, rainbow-colored ball of light roll across the floor where we had been playing. I was terrified. I was only seven years old at the time, so I had no idea what it was. It was the scariest thing that has ever happened to me. The ball rolled past us in the living room and blew up with the loudest bang I ever heard.

When Dad returned home, he noticed the black burn mark on the floor where the ball exploded, and he saw me shaking with fear. He was astonished when he heard my explanation, but he agreed with what I saw. In my adult life, in America, I have read about ball lightning that can enter an open door or window. To this day, I still have a lingering fear of lightning and thunder.

When I came to America, I believed I left my reasons to be afraid back in Lebanon. There was no one to punish me if I didn't follow orders to the tee. There was no one to pick me up by my hair and throw me to the floor if I didn't understand something right away, no one to call me a dummy, to tell me that I didn't deserve to eat, that it was better to give my food to the animals. I wouldn't have to cringe while seeing my

Mother slapped and thrown to the floor. Yes, I'm talking about my Dad. He didn't follow me to America, but the damage he caused to my self-esteem, my confidence, my trust, and my whole outlook about love and relationships followed me. Anger and fear were imbedded deep within me from his cruel treatment. Not only did I have fears in school that affected my ability to focus and excel, my whole life was affected in some way by my childhood memories. I couldn't escape the grip my Dad still had on my life. Even today, everyday occurrences can make me anxious and fearful.

My fear often would be a spontaneous reaction to an event that reminded me of a fearful childhood experience. This occurred while Omar and I was on a camping trip to Niagara Falls, Canada. It sounded adventurous and I was excited to go. It was also cheaper to camp than get a hotel. As luck would have it, there was a thunderstorm and lightning brewing the evening we arrived. We were in a small tent that kept us dry while pouring rain and lightning came down. I was terrified to the bone. I panicked and screamed to Omar, "What are we going to do?" He said calmly, "We will be safe here." I screamed, "I am not going to stay in the tent!" He told me it was safer if we stayed low and dry. I yelled, "I'm not staying!" and with that, I unzipped the door and darted out of the tent, with Omar chasing me and pleading for me to come back. He yelled, "Where are you going?" I said, "I don't know, but I don't want to stay in the tent!" We were both soaking wet from head to toe. Finally, we reached a pavilion where we could sit out the storm. I don't know if it was a fear of the unknown, or fear of being struck by lightning, or just plain fear. When the storm passed, we headed back to the tent and slept for a few hours. The next day was beautiful, and we enjoyed the rest of our camping trip.

When I look back at another example of my lifetime fear of storms and lightning, I find this story to be a bit humorous. It was the summer of 2000. I always took my Mom to her doctor's appointments. This day, the sky looked dark and threatening, and I was afraid we would get caught in the storm. My Mom needed to keep her dialysis appointment. I prayed the storm would hold off until we got back home. We made it to her appointment without an incident, but on the way home, the threat became real. The rain started pouring down so hard that I couldn't see. I pulled to the side of the road to wait until the weather improved, but it only got worse. I began yelling at the top of my lungs, "Oh my God! Oh my God! What are we going to do?!" My Mom quietly stared at me like I was nuts.

Lightning started to hit around us, and the rain was so fierce I couldn't see out of the windows. I panicked! I rolled the window down, and with the rain peppering my face, began screaming to passing cars, "Help! Help! Help!" as loud as I could. My Mom finally spoke up and asked, "What are you doing?? No one is going to hear you!! What do you want someone to help you with?" I said, "I don't know. I just want help." She said, "Are you nuts? Amira, we are only two blocks from home! Just keep driving!" I asked, "Do you want me to keep going?" She said, "Yes, we will be alright." I came to my senses and continued home, feeling foolish.

On another occasion, ominous-looking, black, rolling cloud formations appeared above the lake where we lived. They were moving and rolling very fast, about 50 feet above the water. I had never seen such ugly, threatening, rolling clouds in my life. I yelled to Omar, "Let's go to the basement!" I headed straight to the basement, screaming at Omar all the way. I felt something terrible was going to happen. I looked back and found Omar wasn't behind me. I yelled again, "Omar, where are you??" He didn't respond because he had headed upstairs to get his camera so he could capture pictures of the unusual clouds. When he came back to the main floor, he responded, "I'm taking pictures! I've never seen clouds like this either, and I don't want to miss this opportunity!" As it turned out, the clouds formed into a tornado about five miles down the road. Maybe this time, Omar was a little bit more nuts than I was!

I can't believe what I saw

We decided to sell our dream house we had built in West Bloomfield, MI, before Omar retired. It was almost 5,000 sq. ft, and too big for us to live in after he retired. We bought a beautiful, smaller house in south Florida to prepare for our move. There was not enough room for all of our furniture in the new house, so we sold most of it and stored what we planned to take to Florida. Moving from our dream home that we designed and built, on a beautiful lake, was not easy. I didn't know how to handle my emotions and mental stress that surrounded me. The pressure was overtaking my positive thinking.

It was late July 2019 when we began moving furniture and personal items into a storage facility. It was depressing to see my carefully placed decorations in boxes. For many treasures, it would be the last time I would be able to enjoy them. I had filled our home with all of my favorite pictures, dolls, vases, and rugs. To see all of them loaded into a truck broke my heart. I am still grieving today. On the way back from our first trip to unload furniture at the storage facility, I was feeling extremely exhausted and thought it would be a good idea to rest my eyes for a little while. It was about a 15 minute drive back to our home.

I reclined in the car seat and closed my eyes to meditate and calm myself. Immediately, a tall man in the sky appeared. It seemed as though he was about a half-mile away. The sky was a pure, vivid blue with no clouds. I began to feel very relaxed. His face was too far away for me to recognize who it was. As soon as I questioned, in my thoughts, who is this man, his face moved closer to me until I could see facial features. I could see a beautiful, peaceful face, with long hair and a beard. A voice in my head told me this is Jesus, and I felt warmth flow all over my body. When we arrived in our driveway, I awoke from my slumber and returned to reality.

A few days later, we made a second trip to the storage facility, which was just as traumatic for me as the first trip. Again, I was exhausted and decided to rest on the way home. I closed my eyes, and a few moments later, I saw the image of a man's face above a faraway mountain. A voice told me to look up. I didn't open my eyes, but I saw a white cloud develop in a circular shape in the sky. The beautiful, circular-shaped cloud started to move closer and closer to me, slowly transforming into a huge, white rose. The rose appeared bigger and bigger as it moved toward me. Eventually, the rose came to a stop around me. It was as though I was inside the rose. The man's face was no longer visible to me. I said to myself, "Oh my God, I can't believe what I am seeing." I heard the same voice say, "This rose is yours." I opened my eyes when I got back home, and had this amazing, relaxed feeling. I felt that I wouldn't be afraid of anything because my Guardian Angel will always be there when I need her. I felt power inside of me. This Angel will comfort me when I am feeling scared or worried about the next roadblock or dark tunnel I'll have to traverse.

Omar gives me comfort and support with all I do. He keeps me going and gives his best with everything he does. He continually reminds me: there is light at the end of every tunnel -- remember that!

Appreciation Notes

I want to give my most profound appreciation to my husband and soul mate, who smoothed the speed bumps and removed roadblocks along the way. He spent quality time with me since the day we met, and still does. I feel his warm heart. He is my best friend and my Angel.

I also want to thank Mary Shoucair, my dear friend who gave me light when I was crawling through the darkness. She gave me what I needed when I needed it most. She lived to the age of 96. God rest her soul. I miss her.

I also want to thank my brother, Adnan, who gave me his car when he was leaving the country. This gave me a lift in my self-esteem, and the ability to keep moving down my highway. I will never forget this act of kindness.

I want to thank Wayne County Community College (the Northwest Campus formerly on Greenfield Rd) and friends who seemed to understand what I was going through during my early days in America. They provided support and guidance, and gave me hope and purpose. I didn't feel intimidated or bullied because of my naivety and fear, as I had in other educational institutions. From the bottom of my heart, "THANK YOU."

I also want to thank my Mom for giving me comforting childhood memories. She kept me from going crazy from my Dad's treatment. My Mom gave me many reasons to live, to keep crawling, a desire to give to others. When Mom passed away in 2001, my nieces and her grandchildren brought Kit-Kat bars to the funeral. Mama, your body is no longer with us, but your spirit lives on in the hearts of everyone you've touched. You still live among us. God rest your soul.

Last, but not least, Hanan and Majdi Akra, of DocuMall, in Toledo, OH for making my book readable. Without their help to unscramble the first draft of my life story, a reader probably would have stopped reading after the prologue. The work they did was far beyond any editing that could have been done by any other source. A heartfelt thanks to both of you. The energy and enthusiasm you have put into my books are so appreciated. God Bless!

Conclusion

This book highlights my life and experiences. I hope it can serve as an inspiration to others. I did not write this book to gain sympathy from anyone. Whatever happened in the past is the past. Many people are going through difficult times, but if you are determined, you can succeed. I went through many struggles in my life. I had a rough childhood, struggled in America, got a divorce, and endured severe health issues. Through it all, I kept crawling. I let nothing stand in my way.

Today life is good. I am excited that Siham Awada Jaafar, host and producer of WDHT TV Community Connection and "Off the Cuff," interviewed me on her show to talk about my "Amazing Activities."

Nada and her husband, Ali, live in a beautiful home in Dearborn. Their daughter, Amira, is married to a wonderful man. She is studying to become a doctor. Their younger daughter, Aya, is living in New York and works as a film producer in the movie industry.

Omar recently retired from Magna. We sold our dream home in West Bloomfield, MI, and now reside in south Florida.

The main message I want people to learn is this: No matter what hits you in life, keep going forward. Whether you crawl, walk or run down your highway, keep moving forward. Never, never give up!

Biography

Author of four books:

Healing the Wounds of Alzheimer's Disease

ABC's of Activities for Alzheimer's (Award-winning)

Activity Techniques that Heal the Wounds of Alzheimer's

Amazing Activities for Low Function and Caregiver Guide

Credentials

BA - Management of Human Resources (Spring Arbor University)

Certified Activities Consultant (NCCAP)

Certified CE Educator (NCCAP)

Certified Reiki Master and Teacher

Certified Dementia Practitioner (CDP)

Trained Activity Directors in facilities

NADA Certified Auricular Acupuncturist

Produced an educational Video for Alzheimer's Activities Training

Certified Laughter Leader - World Laughter Tour

Provide certified workshops for caregivers & professionals (1.5, 2 & 4 hrs.) and 8 hr. online course

Taught Nursing students & caregivers at Henry Ford Community College

Participated in the Alzheimer's Association's Public Policy Forum in Washington, D.C.

President of Alzheimer Activities Service, providing activities for individuals and groups with Alzheimer's for more than 20 yrs.

Awards

Michigan Association of Activity Professionals (MAAP) Excellence Award for Demonstrating Outstanding Excellence in the Activities Profession

National Mature Media Award Program - Silver Award Winner

World Laughter Tour-"Laffayette Award" for Back to the Future" Advanced Scholars Workshop

Presentations

AAHPERD National Convention

Alzheimer's Association Caregiver Education Workshop for students at Wayne State University

Blue Cross/Blue Shield of Michigan's Conference on "Aging Successfully"

Madonna University Gerontology students (4hr) "Activity in Aging."

Ohio Health Care Association's Convention

Michigan Association of Activity Professionals Annual Convention

Henry Ford Hospital, Hospice In-service Volunteers American Society on Aging

National Certification Council of Activity Professionals National Association of Activity Professionals

West Bloomfield Rotary Club Matrix Human Services

World Laughter Tour Convention Macklin Intergenerational Institute

Presented workshops to hundreds of caregivers and activity professionals throughout the country

Memberships

National Acupuncture Detoxification Detox Association

The Alzheimer's Association

Michigan Association of Activity Professionals

National Association of Activity Professionals

American Society on Aging

World Laughter Tour

Senior Coordination Aging Network (SCAN) of Oakland County

Association of Applied Therapeutic Humor (AATH)

My Hero

OMAR

Omar is my husband, my hero
And my best friend

You raised me up
To more than I can be

You raised me up

When no one was there for me
I thought I am strong,
I can walk far enough to find my dream

This is me now!

You raised me up when I did not know me
my heart was lost and did not know you
but you did not give up on me
You raised me up to more than I can be
You found my soul and fell in love with me
Your love guided me.
And you planted seeds in my heart
And your wisdom raised me up
Now I can walk on the mountain with no fear
Now I am living my dream,
you raised me up for the dream I dream

This was me when
we first met

Your girl Amira   Thursday, June 07, 2012